DATE DUE			
APR 8 1989			
MAY 1 7 1993			
SEP 2 6 2003			
SEP 2 6 2003			

The
Indigo Bunting

Edna St. Vincent Millay

The
Indigo Bunting

A Memoir of Edna St. Vincent Millay

by

VINCENT SHEEAN

HARPER & BROTHERS
New York

To the Worthingtons, Katherine and Lyman.

INDIGO BUNTING (Passerina Cyanea). *Range:* Breeds from North Dakota and New Brunswick to Texas and Georgia. Winters from Mexico to Panama, and in Cuba. *Habitat:* Brushy country, abandoned pastures, roadsides. *Identification:* Breeding male our only small bird—length, about 5½ inches—that is *blue all over.* Female, thick-billed, brown, with some bluish wash. *Voice:* a sweet, delicate *tsing-tsing-tsing, chipper-ipper-ee.* Likely to be recognized because bird sings in heat of day, and late summer, when most other bird-voices are still.

—AUDUBON: *The Birds of America.*

CONTENTS

The
Indigo Bunting

I

The Indigo Bunting

MIGRATORY birds do not pause often or long on the
farm in Vermont where I live. Perhaps it is not at the
required distance for a day's journey on either the northward or
the southward flight, and perhaps its climate does not invite
repose either in spring or autumn when the birds are on the
wing. For these or other reasons, including deficient observation
on my own part, I have not noticed many visitors of this kind.

One day, it is true, I saw the scarlet tanager on my own farm.
I was coming up from the village of Barnard with Mr. Walter
Miller, the owner of the general store there, who was driving me
home because my car was out of order. Mr. Miller suddenly
stopped his truck a few feet down the road and said in a voice
of wonder: "Now what is that bird? I've never seen a bird like
that here. Or anywhere else. What is it?"

By the side of the road, on the pasture fence, there was sitting
a small, pert blaze of color. I did not recognize it, knowing little
of birds then or now, and we both stared at the animal while it

confidently stared back. After a few minutes of this mutual inspection the bird flew over our truck to the other side of the road and perched on a branch, adopting another point of view without any slackening of curiosity.

"It looks like some of the birds I've seen in India," I told Mr. Miller. "Perhaps it's come from India to pay a visit. You can't tell about birds."

The bird stayed on the farm for some hours on that day and then vanished. When I looked into the invaluable Audubon, which I had acquired some months before as a Christmas present, it was easy enough to identify the scarlet tanager. He has not since appeared on the farm so far as I know.

The state of my knowledge about migratory birds at the time can be measured by this failure to recognize the tanager, which is surely of all birds the easiest to name. Nor can it be said that I have learned very much in the years since then. What little I know was acquired from Miss Edna St. Vincent Millay, rare woman and poet, rare poet and woman, who had spent the secret hours of dawn upon them for many years. The kinship she acknowledged by her habitual action toward them was, it appeared to me, amply confessed by the birds themselves in their behavior toward her, although Edna laughed at the idea. According to her, they would have behaved in the same way toward anybody who fed them. This I took leave to doubt then as I do now, on the simple ground of probability. What I actually saw myself, and many others have seen, between Edna and the birds (although much was never seen) was improbable enough; that it should occur with any frequency, or to "anybody who feeds them," is beyond credence.

The Indigo Bunting

Edna St. Vincent Millay lived at a house called Steepletop near the village of Austerlitz in New York State. She had, by her own peculiar magic, the capacity to inspire devotion and thus was upheld through life by many unquestioning friendships—friendships with men and women who asked nothing but the privilege of occasionally sharing the edge of her existence. This was about all they did get, but it was enough, since those who appreciated her in this particular way felt that through her they reached some region not ordinarily accessible —somewhere near the gates of wonder, perhaps, on the other side of every day.

Among these was Esther Adams (wife of F.P.A.) who had grown into the habit of spending her birthday at Steepletop. It was a privilege she regarded highly and would not have missed for anything in her power; she had been to Steepletop on every June fourth for a considerable number of years. Edna Millay and her husband, Eugen Boissevain, were very fond of Esther, whom they called "Tess," and although for the greater part of the year they seldom saw Esther or any other friend, the fourth of June had become a fixed festival for them, too. They looked forward to it and adopted certain rituals—such as the Brahms-Haydn *Variations*—which came to be repeated year after year. On almost every occasion this birthday was celebrated by the three of them, Edna and Esther and Eugen. There was seldom any other person present.

For June fourth, 1948, they asked me to come along. I took a train out to Westport from New York and Esther picked me up there and drove me on up to Steepletop. (This was on June third.) The day was bright enough when we left Westport but it soon turned into a thoroughgoing example of the dripping summer downpour, with visibility extremely limited and not much prospect of relief. We got to the village of Austerlitz in this deluge and as I remember it let up a bit just as we turned off to the house, Steepletop. It was a white frame house not much different from the older farmhouses of upper New York and all New England, except that it did seem to be deeper in trees than most. This circumstance, which must have made it bosky and umbrageous in other weather, gave it a most melancholy atmosphere in the unceasing rain. During that and the two following days there was little or no respite from the downpour; when it did briefly stop it was for a still, clear sunlessness which was just as damp in feeling as the rain itself. And of course the thick crowding trees never ceased to drip whether the rain was actually falling or not. I remember remarking about a year later to Esther, when she spoke of that strange and wonderful week end, that it had been burdened by bad weather. She said: "Weather? Was there any weather?"

From the moment we arrived, it was clear that Edna was in good health, good temper, good spirits, and good form. She could vary exceedingly. At times she was so afflicted by self-consciousness and dislike for the external world that she could hardly utter a word; I have seen her cringe—this was in New York, in a crowd—actually physically cringe, when she felt herself being observed. She felt free at Steepletop, where every blade of grass was a familiar, and there was not the slightest danger that anybody would come near the door. There was no telephone in the house (when it became necessary to telephone, somebody,

usually Eugen, made an excursion to the general store in Austerlitz). Her dislike for company was so well understood both
among the neighbors and among her distant friends that nobody
would have thought of going to Steepletop at all without an
invitation or at least a permission given in advance. She had
thus established the place as a sort of refuge in which she could
and did, for many months on end, see no human being except
Eugen and John, Mr. Pinnie, the farmer who was, silently but
permanently, her worshiper. (She had, however, many other
companions, as will appear.)

She met us at the door with a cheerful welcome and led us
into the long room with the big plain window at the end. Her
preferred chair, where she most often sat, was beside this big
square window and so placed in the corner that she could at all
times see what was going on outside the window as well as in
the room. This was in the late afternoon and there was still
light of a rather damp and subdued nature. Very soon after we
had come into the room, almost before we had finished the first
flurry of welcome and arrival-chatter, I saw a small bird of the
most dazzling blue alight on the window sill and depart.

"What in the world," I asked, "is that? Did you see?"

"Of course," Edna said in that deep, serious voice which was
characteristic throughout the time I knew her. "Don't you know
him? That is the indigo bunting."

"Indigo bunting?"

"He is on his way to the north. He has been in Central
America, or perhaps in South America. Do you mean to say
that you have never seen an indigo bunting?"

I was abashed a little, as we always are at exhibitions of our own ignorance, but thought I might as well confess at once and get it over. I told her about the scarlet tanager on the farm in Vermont a week or so before. She was rather shocked but also rather amused.

"The scarlet tanager should be about the most easily recognized of all migratory birds," she said, not too censoriously. "He comes here fairly often. He isn't here just at the moment."

"Why do they come here?"

"Because I feed them, of course," she said.

Eugen was giving us a drink, his huge and friendly and ever-remembered form moving about the room from Esther to Edna to me. He laughed.

"She feeds them!" he said. "She runs a hotel for birds. She's up and at it every morning before dawn."

"Another one!" I said, startled. "And another! Now what's that?"

A big, brilliant bird had alighted and was followed by another. They looked us over with none of the hasty dislike of their all-blue predecessor.

"That's the rose-breasted grosbeak," Edna said rather indifferently. "There are quite a few of them this year. They aren't at all rare. Do you mean to say you've never seen one?"

The rose-breasted grosbeak did not seem shy, but remained for mutual inspection (one of them did, that is) for some minutes. I think this is another bird I shall always recognize hereafter. It became evident to my rather slow perceptions that this was why a big, square window had been put at the end of the long room: so that the birds could look in at Edna and Edna could look out at the birds. This established the daylong interest of that end of the room; the fireplace was in the middle on the left, and we needed it that day; two grand pianos stood at the other end, near the door which led to hall, dining room, and kitchen. Edna saw me watching the window with, no doubt, some element of the astonishment I felt. The comings and goings, the general activity, were indeed considerable and I had never seen anything of the kind before.

"Those are only finches," she said. "They aren't remarkable but they're pretty. Various kinds."

"I can't understand it," I told her. "There are so many. Why do they come to this window?"

"For food, I told you," she scolded. "There's food on the window sill. And do you see that round table there, outside under the tree? There's food there too."

"How do they know, when they come from so far?"

"How can I tell you?"

And then, as conversation shifted again and the finches disappeared, for one blinding moment the indigo bunting came back. He took a peck or two at the window sill, seemed to glance once penetratingly into the room, and was off in a blue rush. The swiftness of this took my breath away.

"He doesn't like a great crowd of people standing round and staring at him," she said. "There is something to be said for his point of view. He lives not far off, you see, up there in that nearest tree, and it's quite easy for him to come back when there aren't so many observers."

At this point or somewhere near it Esther said it was time for us to drop our luggage and wash for dinner. We got into raincoats, as the rain had just started again, and went over to the guesthouse on the other side of the path, a little distance away, Eugen puffing and blowing as our guide. It was a wooden structure that looked in the dark as if it were on stilts (in reality there was a garage beneath); it had outside stairs, and contained one big room, a studio where work was sometimes done by both of them: this was for Esther. A small room at the top of the stairs was for me. By the time Eugen had settled us in, the rain had become a downpour again, as it was to be throughout the night. We sat and talked for a little and then did what we had to do before making the dash back to the house.

We had dinner quite late that night. In the first place there seemed no end to the extension—forward, backward, and in all directions—to which any such conversation with Miss Millay might be subject. I had never fallen upon this particular mood with her before, in our few meetings over the years. She had seemed reluctant to talk much, or for long at a time, or to engage in any very animated discussion, or to pursue a subject with the particular animosity of dispute which engenders lively response and long consideration. Now we fell, by what accident I cannot remember, upon Keats and Shelley, by way of some chance remark about the happiness or unhappiness of poets. Edna asked me which of the two I regarded as more unhappy, and I said Keats. This was the signal for her to take the opposite point of view with such vigor, wit, and beauty of language as I have seldom heard. Her memory for poetry was, as is well known, phenomenal, and she had also cultivated it—she memorized poetry deliberately when she was sick abed, or alone in a train, the way other people read magazines or play patience—and in the result she could command page after page of Keats and Shelley at will. Since her voice, so deep and clear and filled with melody, was peculiarly suited to the recalling of poetic lines, the quotations with which she filled her talk had never sounded quite like that to me before. I did not surrender my point of view, nor do I now: in so far as I understand them Shelley was not capable of the deep human unhappiness of Keats, nor had he any reason to feel, as Keats did, the gratuitous insults of fate. But Edna's command of the poetry of both, and her multitude of reasons for suffering—by which Shelley's ethereal flight itself became a kind of unhappiness—left me vanquished in the immediate argument.

(I was afterward told by an old friend of hers that in the days when she spent many an hour and day in such talk with her friend Elinor Wylie it had been the other way round—Edna's sympathy was deeper for Keats and her friend's for Shelley—but that was twenty-five years before.)

It must have been half-past ten or later when we sat down to dinner, and although I remember that the dinner was excellent I could never take oath upon what was in it. Edna had changed into something which I remember as being blue and trailing; Esther Adams tells me it was that indeed, and "deep aquamarine satin," as well, and also that it was new (or anyhow Esther had never seen it before).

She had brushed out her red hair until it surrounded her face and gave it the spritelike quality that is to be seen in some portraits and earlier photographs. At dinner we were not restricted to birds and poets; indeed not; most of the talk was about food, and how best to prepare this or that dish. I have seen some letters of Edna's to a friend in Florida (the wife of an Italian) which were almost entirely about spaghetti. I do not know how much she knew about cooking; when I was there Eugen seemed to do it all; but there could be no doubt about how she liked the taste of food.

It was extremely late indeed when we left the long room with the two pianos at one end and the bird window at the other. The subject of Gerard Manley Hopkins came up, as it often did with her, and she vented a little spleen on the late Robert Bridges for having, as she said, spoiled the sense of one of Hopkins' best sonnets, the one on Patience. Her explanation, given in that resonant voice, should have been perfectly clear, but in fact on the following day I had to ask her to repeat it. Her animation, her voice, and at times her very extraordinary beauty—not the beauty of every day but apart—did somewhat take away from the full, precise attention her words deserved. Consequently it required careful reiteration in the blue light of the morning after for me to understand what Bridges had done.

This was, I am sure, rather usual in the experience of Edna Millay's friends. Her own personality got in the way of what she was saying, so that they very often could not remember a day or so later what it was that had struck them so much. We walked with her to the foot of the stairs that night (so late that I dare not trust my own memory as to the hour) and I remember saying to her: "Now are you going to get up and feed the birds after this?"

An indignant flash: "Of course I am! How dare you suggest that I won't?"

Esther and I walked down the dripping path to the guest house through something like a flood. It hardly seemed possible that the guest house—or, for that matter, Steepletop itself—could survive much more rain of this torrential kind. We talked very little before turning in, and during that very little, Esther remarked that Edna had tonight been "just like the old days," without the agonized shyness and multiple terrors of recent years.

It poured all night and most of the morning, but by ten o'clock, when I made my way over to Steepletop, it was beginning to let up a little. I found Esther, Eugen, and Edna all in the kitchen, just finishing last night's dishes, while the coffee steamed away in the pot and eggs danced in the skillet. It was a cheerful farm kitchen and Mr. Pinnie, the farmer from down the hill, came bringing wood and exchanging a spare word or two.

We had breakfast in the kitchen and before it was over Edna had returned to Keats and Shelley. But then it was time—when the dishes had been washed—for the Brahms-Haydn *Variations*, which Edna and Esther performed at the two pianos with great seriousness and attention to line and detail, even though Edna said she had not played them since the last time "Tess" had a birthday. They both put on their glasses and watched the music with hawklike intensity, and every once in a while one or the other would call a halt and start over again from a given point, as is the manner of people the world over when they love the music and are not professional performers. Then there was some other music, and we talked about German songs, in which—as in all the literatures—Edna had her favorites. More and more, in all conversation, there was a sort of enlarging glimpse of her range. When she spoke of Mozart, for example, or Beethoven, it was not in the manner of salon talk, but with an artist's knowledge of what it was that set the works apart. And even among songs, both in French and in German, although the chatter was light enough and inconsecutive enough, it was obvious that she had known them well in order to be able to pick her way amongst them so securely. She or Esther played a phrase of this and a phrase of that; Esther told her about my liking to "read" German *Lieder*—i.e., to sing them in so far as I could do so when an accompanist fell into my clutches—and it appeared at once that she had long indulged in the same form of reading. She, of course, could read them and sing them to herself, which is the only way of knowing a song.

The weather turned almost bright—as bright as it was going to be that week end—and Esther wandered off to the vegetable garden with Eugen, leaving me with Edna. We returned to the other end of the room, by the bird window, equipped with small, shallow glasses of New York State champagne, which was our tipple, mild but constant, for that day. I asked her to tell me again, so that I could remember, what Bridges had done to the Hopkins sonnet on Patience. She told me.

The Bridges version is as follows

The Indigo Bunting

Patience, hard thing! the hard thing but to pray,
But bid for, Patience is! Patience who asks
Wants war, wants wounds; weary his times, his tasks;
To do without, take tosses, and obey.
    Rare patience roots in these, and, these away,
Nowhere. Natural heart's ivy, Patience masks
Our ruins of wrecked past purpose. There she basks
Purple eyes and seas of liquid leaves all day.

We hear our hearts grate on themselves: it kills
To bruise them dearer. Yet the rebellious wills
Of us we do bid God bend to him even so.
    And where is he who more and more distils
Delicious kindness?—He is patient. Patience fills
His crisp combs, and that comes those ways we know.

I have given it in full, as Edna said it in full on that day. Her accusation against Bridges, however, depends entirely on the comma in line six after the word "ivy." Bridges admitted that the comma was his, introduced when he prepared the Hopkins poems for publication in 1918. It is to be assumed that he thought this was the only proper way to make sense out of his dead friend's sonnet.

But Edna's case is that Bridges must have misunderstood his friend altogether—as seems quite likely anyhow—because of this comma. What the comma establishes, she said, is one single kind of patience, to which Bridges gives the initial capital letter. (Hopkins did not.) Hopkins was writing of two kinds of patience. One was the hard thing which wants war, wants wounds, to take tosses and obey. This is rare patience; rare patience roots in these and nowhere else. The other kind of patience ("Natural heart's ivy Patience") is a sort of feather bed for ruin, a covering-up, a satisfied self-decay.

These are not Edna's words. She did not explain too much. She did it by means of accenting the poetry itself correctly, which I despair of reproducing on the printed page. The explanation as given above is in my words, but it is her meaning, because I was at great pains to get it clear, and she said the poem to me, in her deep, penetrating voice, at least seven or eight times in her way and in the Bridges way. If you read the poem in the way Bridges understood it (with one Patience, capital P, and with the comma setting off "Natural heart's ivy") then the duality or dichotomy which Hopkins had in mind, the theme of his poem, is completely lost. The sestet states with the utmost clarity Hopkins' preference for "rare patience" over the other kind of patience, and his prayer to God to take tosses and obey.

In other words, I was convinced then and am now that Edna proved her point completely by the sense of the whole poem, and Bridges, in spite of the great piety and devotion with which he edited and published his dead friend's vagrant verses, did not truly understand them. As Edna recited the lines, over and over, subtly different every time, I thought how unlucky it was for all of us that she had never undertaken that book she once thought about, a book of prose—it would have been her only real one— an interpretation of Hopkins' poetry.

By what transition I no longer remember, but we were back to Keats and Shelley again before long. And then Esther and Eugen came into the room from their walk. Esther's fair hair with reddish lights in it had been considerably blown by the wind and she was also a bit bedewed by the dripping trees; she came into the room with the eager and breathless manner which is somehow characteristic of her, as if that which she had just reluctantly left was not half so exciting as that she now expected.

"Tess," said Edna, "you look like the locks of the approaching storm."

"Ah," said Esther, pleased, "I know what it is but I don't remember where it comes."

"Now, please," I said. "Tell me what it is. I don't have that kind of memory at all."

Edna said:

> *Angels of rain and lightning there are spread*
> *On the blue surface of thine airy surge,*
>   *Like the bright hair uplifted from the head*
> *Of some fierce Maenad, even from the dim verge*
>   *Of the horizon to the zenith's height,*
> *The locks of the approaching storm.*

Eugen and Esther and I all cried out with pleasure after she had said these lines. When she wished to give enough power to her voice it was as thrilling as the voice of the very greatest actress or singer. Suddenly, for some reason, at that moment she wished to give power to her voice. It was a visceral experience. We pleaded for more, and then—probably because it was Esther's birthday—she recited the "Ode to the West Wind" in its entirety. The range of expression, within severe limits (for she did not "act" at all) was astonishing. With the voice alone, without gesture or movement or expression of the face, she remembered the poem and gave it to us anew as if we had never heard it before in our lives. And this extraordinary re-creation had nothing whatever to do with the arts of theater, dramatic reading, or anything else of a factitious kind. It was for poetry alone. One could hear precisely where the lines broke and rose and fell, like the sea, and where the mood itself grew faint or strong with the flow of sense and feeling.

Esther and Eugen went away again, perhaps to see about lunch. (I was incapable of moving.) I heard afterward that they had both been so stirred by Edna's voice in the Ode that they could not remain in the room. She had not done such a thing for a long time. She continued to talk to me about Shelley, now no longer within the framework of our long argument of the night before, but simply about the poet and how he beat his wings, and why: his life and song and death. (He died in the sea, too, as she had wished to die.) She was trying to convey something to me about him, and to do so she did another miraculous thing: she said the entire "Hymn to Intellectual Beauty." This, however, was not stormy like the other. It was said in the quietest of voices, reflectively, reminiscently, almost as if she had herself written it a long time ago.

> *The awful shadow of some unseen Power*
> *Floats though unseen among us,—*

We had lunch on the little flagged terrace outside the kitchen. The sun had flickered out for a bit, and remained bright enough for the whole of the meal before it clouded over again. We talked of food and friends, and told stories. After lunch, at coffeetime, mindful of the terrace and seeing no ash trays, I put a cigarette out in my coffee cup and received a sharp scolding from Edna. Somebody would have to wash up after me; this was wicked behavior, antisocial and unaesthetic, I gathered; I was more surprised and amused than anything else, although she was in fact quite serious about it. We collaborated in washing the dishes and then wandered down into the garden on the other side of the house, the side of the approach from the road.

It was a tangled garden with a pool, narrow and stagnant enough to belong to an Italian villa or a college at Cambridge. Flowers would be here, there, and there, later on: Edna told us something about them. Now it was all wet green and dripping. At one end of the pool was a little covered bar with a roof over it and stools in front of it. At the other end, embedded now in greenery and weeds, was a marble torso, pleasantly discolored by time, which suggested Greece. Somewhere in that thicket there was a nest from which the mother bird sallied forth angrily at us, coming and going nervously all the time we were there. Edna told us the bird's name and habit and eventually decided upon our departure so as not to arouse any more of its anxiety over the young, which were no doubt very young.

The dripping green reminded me—with other associations, too—of the country around Grasmere and Windermere. Dinah, my wife, had gone with me to the Lakes a few years before and we had visited the tiny cottage where Wordsworth lived with Dorothy. We had loved the country, wet as it was, and on one providentially clear evening we had walked out on the pier from the hotel at Lake Windermere and, overcome by the placid stillness of the water and the stars, had taken to our backs, supine, to look up into the floor of heaven. When we got up to go in we were both of us covered from head to toe with bird droppings.

"So much," I said to Edna, "for your poets and your birds! See what they do to you!"

"Yes, they do," she said, accepting it, and began to talk about Wordsworth and his particular countryside. While we teetered on our stools in front of the rain-soaked bar, and Eugen pretended to be barman with the remnants of the New York State champagne, she told us about the drovers that passed over the road from north to south in the Lake country, and quoted lines from poems by Wordsworth. The effect of quotation—which can be the most wearisome of impediments in some cases—was altogether special with her, because the lines appeared to come from within and were never used as applied ornament. Usually when she said a line or lines of poetry her voice and intonation would give it the quality of discovery, as if it came either from her own depths or through them, but not at all from an outside repository to which others might have access at will. Thus she said some lines from "The Waggoner" and, finding that we did not know the work or had forgotten it, proceeded to tell us about Benjamin the Waggoner and his horses and his wain "along the banks of Rydal Mere." She delighted in some lines, particularly when it appears that Benjamin the Waggoner had once been welcomed to the Grasmere Vale by a drink at the pub called the Dove and Olive-Bough; where now (alas for Benjamin!) Wordsworth lived.

> . . . *a Poet harbours now,*
> *A simple water-drinking Bard.*

The Indigo Bunting

The poem is long and she did not say a great deal of it, but it was enough to fill out the most vivid sketch of those misted valleys and soft green hills.

Then, as I have already said, the indignant mother bird in the nest above the pool succeeded in persuading Edna that we should depart, which we did. She and Esther went back to the house for a session (it was *Esther's* birthday!) and Eugen and I, after a visit to the water pump at the foot of the garden, went our several ways to snatch at a little sleep.

When I returned to the long room in the house it was evening and the birds were in full attendance. All the ones I had seen the evening before were there, and others whose names I forget. There were several varieties of finches, gold and yellow and purple and greenish-yellow, who were as familiar and distinguishable to Edna as Chinese are to Chinese. (I had reminded myself of the foreigners in China who used to say: "All Chinese look alike to me.") We sat and talked about birds for a while and I told her, as I had once before, that I thought she was instinctively pantheistic and had some relationship to these creatures. She denied it, of course, but when I asked how she could explain the behavior of sea gulls toward her, she grew a little thoughtful. She then told me the story of a winter sparrow that once flew by mistake into her room, upstairs in this house, and of the difficulties she experienced in calming the bird enough to release him. He had in fact become almost tame by the time she could get him into her hands and out of the window.

Interspersed with the talk about birds there was a good deal about various Hindu beliefs, the rebirth of souls, the identity of

19

all souls, and the inviolability of life. I was standing up, walking up and down the room, and she was in her usual chair so that she could see both the room and the birds. I suddenly saw the indigo bunting at the window and plunged across the room to look (it was getting dark).

"There he is!" I said. "There he is again! No—no—he's gone."

"Of course he's gone," Edna said. "What do you expect? Birds don't like buffaloes. You're a buffalo. Don't go charging at him like that. Just sit down and be quiet and he will come back again."

I sat down in the chair opposite and we did not say much for a bit until the bird came back. In a sense not easily explicable I should have been grievously disappointed (not to say hurt) if the bird had not come back. He returned, blazing blue even in this light, and, observing no disturbance within, pecked at his food and looked us over. He was then joined by another and then another, all males, all unmitigated blue. Edna talked in a low tone about the habits of this particular creature, who is, of course, not in the least rare, and had been well known to her for many years. It was only my own ignorance that made it seem strange.

Eugen and Esther came back; the lights went on; Eugen put wood on the fire. It was cold for June.

That night we all four talked until very far into the night. There was more music and talk of music; there were stories and jokes and anecdotes; the birds and the poets were never away for long. I remember asking Edna whether it was true that the

North American hummingbird cadged a lift on the back of the wild duck in its annual migration, and she said this was perfect nonsense. (I had heard it in Vermont, where there are many hummingbirds in summer.) She said the only example she had ever seen of this particular sort of parasitism—cadging a lift—was among fish: there is a sort of fish which attaches itself to the side of (imagine!) a shark, and thus voyages with no expenditure of energy. This she had seen in Florida.

On the following morning the rain was more torrential than ever. I wanted to get back to Vermont and Esther to New York. It was finally decided that after luncheon Eugen would drive me back to Twin Farms and Esther would drive to Westport. This was much more of a week end than anybody had bargained for (we were to have left the evening before) but weather had taken charge. We had breakfast in the kitchen and I did have a word or two (no more) with Mr. Pinnie, who came again in his taciturn way. At some time or other that morning when I was alone with Edna in the long room we began to talk about Italian poetry. I had already observed that her accent, in the few words I had heard her say in Italian, was extremely good. (She had a special musicopoetic quality for the sound of a language; I do not say that she could have ordered a meal in a restaurant, but she could say a line of poetry in Italian or French, or German, Latin, or Greek.) We were talking of the sonnets of Petrarch. I remarked that the beautiful sonnet on the nightingale—

> *Quel rosignuol che si soave piagne*
> *forse suoi figli o sua cara consorte—*

proceeded upon exactly the opposite line of being from Keats'
ode: that Petrarch moved from the nightingale to himself to the
generality of mankind, whereas Keats—

> *My heart aches, and a drowsy numbness pains*
> *My sense, as though of hemlock I had drunk—*

moved from himself, through a passage of nostalgia for earlier
lives, to the nightingale and then back to himself. My suggestion
was that the narrowing of the line of being to one's self was
modern in poetry, modern and romantic. I do not know that
Edna really accepted the idea, but she did pick up the Petrarch
sonnet from where I left off and say some more of it—almost all
of it, to my amazement. Then she suddenly rose and said:

"Come with me, I'll show you my poets. We'll look at Petrarch.
We'll look at Dante."

She led me across the hall and up the stairs to a small room
just at the top where there were, in every conceivable sort of
binding and state of repair, all the good poets that have ever
written in English, French, German, Italian, Latin, and Greek.
It did not take up much space, since there are so few good poets.
Some editions were old, and no doubt some were valuable, others
valueless; but all had been read and reread by a poet's eyes. We
found Petrarch's sonnet to the nightingale and she read it. We
found Dante. We even found Racine. The love of poetry, when
it is deep and true as it was with her, is sometimes partisan and
exclusive: those who dwell in Shakespeare cannot abide Racine,
and those who live by Goethe will have nothing to do with Heinrich Heine. To Edna each was good and true and beautiful in a

particular way, so that she excluded nothing and condemned nobody, but took it all to herself as she took the sea and the birds. Even in her garden she did not exclude the so-called weeds, and readers of her poems know how they dwell there.

This was the poetry room, as she called it that day, and I understood afterward that very few persons were ever allowed to enter it. Even at the time I knew that I was singularly honored. She did it for Dante and Petrarch, whom she loved, I think, as much as I do.

There was a good deal of coming and going before lunch, and at one moment I found myself all alone in the long room looking out the window, expecting birds. There were no birds, but my eye fell upon a small oblong book, rather like a notebook, lying on the table. It was much thumbed and used and its heavy paper binding (brown in color) was cracked across. It was called *Bird Guide: Land Birds East of the Rockies,* and was ornamented by a rather faded plump bird drawn and colored on one side. I thought it a book and a book only, and so picked it up. To my surprise, as I looked through it, I saw that it was a species of record which Edna kept of the comings and goings of the birds— not every day by any means, and not scientifically or systematically, but every now and then for a period of years. I looked at one or two pages. There was the Chuck-will's widow, which carried at the bottom of the page this penciled note:

Heard—Florida—spring 1936—all night long.

"All" was underlined once, "night" was underlined twice, and "long" was underlined three times.

Some birds were *heard* on such and such a date; some were *seen* on other dates. Most of the precise entries were in the spring or autumn, when the creatures made their annual visits to Steepletop. There was a lot of notation around the page devoted to the rose-breasted grosbeak, our frequent visitor of this week end. I observed that on June 4, 1938—an anniversary: ten years before to the day—two had been first seen feeding on the driveway (sunflower seeds) and singing in the crab-apple tree.

Thanks to her sister Norma I can copy now, so much later, the entry made about the rose-breasted grosbeak on May 24, 1939—still a small penciled scrawl on the same page which contains the data on the bird and its picture:

"May 24, 1939.—Male came to my open window and ate sunflower seeds on the sill very near me. Stayed long time, came again when Ugin was here. Ate about a peck of seeds. Later came into my room for seeds which had scattered in. Stood in middle of my floor and sang!"

There were some signs and symbols on these pages which evidently were a private shorthand. I realized, when I noticed them, that I had no right to be looking at such a book, that it was a sort of secret. I put it down in some embarrassment and when Edna came in, a little later, I told her at once that I had looked at it. She frowned furiously and said: "Now that's really wicked. It's my absolutely private book. You shouldn't do such things." And yet somehow I knew that this time—as distinguished from the time the day before when she had grown angry over the cigarette in the coffee cup—she didn't really mean it.

"Come along," she said, "let's have lunch. You have to get to Twin Farms before dark and it's raining torrents."

We had lunch rather merrily and rather sadly too, because I think we all regretted the end of a strange, fortuitous gathering which, in its incommunicable unity, could not possibly occur again. One meets others repeatedly, as the world says, without ever really meeting. Here we had all met, all four of us, bound in by the incessant rain to a house of magic, caught into it for a day and for ever.

Edna had been calling me "the Buffalo" since yesterday afternoon; now, when Esther said something about the rebirth of the consciousness—another Hindu idea; these came up because I had been in India that year and was writing a book about it—Edna said:

"I know what you were in a previous existence, obviously. It could only have been a buffalo."

"Then you were the indigo bunting?" I asked.

She answered in her deepest voice, very seriously (she had been laughing a second before).

"Yes, perhaps I was the indigo bunting," she said.

I had never then noticed, or at least remembered, that in India the birds perch on the horns and neck of the water buffalo as they do on trees in our country; if I had noticed or remembered I should have told her so, because we had spoken a good deal of India, too, during those days.

The lunch came to an end rather late and Eugen and I made

our departure through the unrelenting downpour. Edna and Esther stood in the doorway and reminded us of everything, the luggage, the route, the weather, and the time.

"Good-by, Buffalo," Edna said.

That was the last time I saw her.

Eugen and I drove off into what seemed a genuinely subaqueous world. It was like traveling in a submarine. It was inevitable that this should come to my mind and that I should say it, which led us off into Dutch submarines, the Dutch Navy and Air Force, and the islands of Indonesia. Eugen was born in The Netherlands of a family which had emigrated from France as Huguenots under Louis XIV, and his family fortunes had been much involved with the Indies—all lost, of course, in the war. He did not know if anything would ever be recovered, but he doubted it. He had gone to the Indies as a very young man, long before he knew Edna or had ever been to America, and they had revisited those wondrous isles years later after their marriage, on a tour they made throughout Asia. We talked of Asia, of the war and the peace, of empires fallen and new states rising. We never mentioned Edna at all, so far as I can remember, except in passing—that is, we did not in any way discuss her. I did remark at one point that her interest in India seemed very great. She had asked me to tell her about the death of Mahatma Gandhi. I had told her everything I could remember about that afternoon, the thirtieth of the preceding January in Delhi, and she had listened with the most tense and tangible act of audition it is possible to imagine. Her listening was so intent that it was like an inhalation.

26

"Yes," Eugen said, plowing on through the walls of water, "she felt something in India. I think she told you so once, at Ragged Island. She felt a difference in the human consciousness. I felt it too, but not as she did. She used to cry; also she was happy there."

That was all there was about Edna during those hours of submarine navigation across the states of New York and Massachusetts.

Eugen was a great hulk of a man, handsome now (at sixty-seven) and must have been remarkable to behold in his youth. He was an excellent driver, as he had to be that afternoon; but he could do everything. The most virile and positive of creatures, he nevertheless served and guarded Edna like the priest of a temple. He cooked, washed dishes, kept house, was gardener and chauffeur, business manager, banker, engineer, and everything else, besides lover and husband and the best friend she ever had. (Or perhaps the best friend anybody ever had.) He retained a Dutch accent but he had been an American for so long that he had little patience with Europe any more, at least politically, and felt the recession of reality from those stricken shores. This did not at all impair his memory of everything he had most enjoyed or admired in Europe, and although he did not communicate too easily, it could be seen that in art and architecture this old world which he had so thoroughly given up had formed his mind. I should have liked to ask, but did not dare, how such a remarkable man could have given his entire life since 1923 to the single purpose of tending one flame. Love, yes: we see it on the wing, usually as a migratory bird, but such love as this is not ordinarily within our purview. I did not ask him that question and am glad I did not. His life supplied the answer in full.

We stopped at Pittsfield for a drink and I telephoned the farm to tell the cook that we were a little late. Dorothy Thompson and Maxim Kopf, my nearest neighbors, were coming to dinner with us and since our telephones are connected I was able to talk also to Dorothy. She said that they would go over to my house and wait for us, and that the weather supplied a good enough excuse for our tardiness.

It never did stop raining. We downed our drinks at Pittsfield (and very welcome they were) and went off on the long last half of the journey. It was well after eight o'clock when we arrived, wet and battered, but Dorothy and Maxim had controlled their appetites and dinner was ready.

We had a very pleasant evening, a good many stories of earlier times and friends, and a little music on the gramophone; then Dorothy and Maxim went home. Dorothy had been a friend of Edna's years ago in Paris and Budapest; Maxim had painted Edna's portrait; naturally a good deal of the talk was about her. We discussed the portrait (Maxim's) which now belongs to the art gallery in Syracuse, New York.

After they had gone, Eugen and I sat in front of the fire until four o'clock in the morning. He told me stories of his youth in Holland, wonderful long stories of snow and skates and dikes and canals, just like the books I read when I was a child. And he also told me, I remember, in beautiful detail, about the time when he and some other Dutch boys made a journey to Rome, and of all

28

the marvels they saw there in the dawn of their time. Then we went to bed and I, as usual after such a session, slept late.

When I got up the next morning Eugen had gone. It was eleven o'clock of a brilliant sunny morning, and the only effect of the long rain was to make the green greener and the blossoms in the orchard in front of my house snowier than ever. (They had not fallen, or few had fallen.) That was the Year of the Great Blossoming on our farm, by the way; it was even more astonishing than 1946, when the old orchard had seemed to me, although bearing no fruit, to be at its best.

"The gentleman has gone," Eva said. "He had a good breakfast, though."

She spoke well of him; he had obviously enlivened his breakfast by talking to her with his usual interest, for he awoke to life every day interested; she had liked him also because he ate a really good breakfast, none of your nonsensical orange juice and coffee but eggs and bacon and all that goes.

"He left a note for you," she said.

I found the note on the hall table amongst the objects usually strewn there. It was a few lines:

Dear Jimmy, I must go because I can't leave Edna alone. Thank you very much. Come again to Steepletop.
The Indigo Bunting is in your hedge.—Eugen.

I puzzled over that for a few minutes. Surely Eugen would not play jokes about such a thing? The old bluebird story, I thought—you wander and wander for what is all the time at home? Surely not.

The Indigo Bunting

I went out into this brilliant morning, across the short sloping lawn to the barberry hedge which stands between it and the road. I had not long to look. On the other side of the hedge, there sat, insolent as billy-be-damned, an unmistakable male indigo bunting, blue all over. The only North American bird that is blue all over.

"Well, you," I said, although very gently because I remembered the buffalo, "have you been there all the time?"

The bird twisted his head brightly to one side and to the other but did not make off at once, as I expected. I stood there quite a while and he endured the scrutiny. When he finally shot up into the air he came right back again on the top of the same hedge, only a little bit farther down.

"It beats me," I said, in the G.I. language which was about all I got out of the war, and went back into the house. But for the whole of that day, the entire day, whenever I went out to look, the indigo bunting was in that hedge, in one place or another, guarding his secret. I told Eva; I told everybody on the farm; I thought it was inexplicable. Nobody else thought so. Very well, they said, there is the indigo bunting—doesn't stop here often.

I cannot explain, either, why I thought it was remarkable, but I did and I do. No other indigo bunting has been seen on this farm since that day, and in fact I have seen no indigo bunting anywhere since then. The bird is not uncommon; but it was on that day that he came here, and nobody fed him, and in spite of his notorious shyness he would not leave that hedge until darkness fell. It is my considered scientific opinion that he was a messenger from Edna, saying that the rain was over.

Eugen died in the following summer, after a surgical operation in Boston. Edna died at Steepletop, at the foot of the stairs leading to the poetry room, at or near dawn on October 19, 1950. In my reconstruction I prefer to think she had been feeding the birds and was on her way to bed. Mr. Pinnie did not find her until many hours later, but the doctors knew how long she had been dead. In the year between Eugen's death and hers I had never dared to go near her, for I had heard, and understood, that she wanted only solitude. It did not in the least surprise me, however, that she died between the birds and the poets, for that is where she had lived, and what are life and death but forms of one another?

I was a little surprised, just the same, to learn only the other day, long after I had begun to write these slight remembrances, that one of the last fragments of poetry she wrote was about the flight of bluebirds, or about blueness. Her sister Norma, reading the last notebook, found it, obviously some parts of a projected sonnet, and considers that it is one of her last, possibly the last. The couplets are:

> *Never before, perhaps, was such a sight—*
> *Only one sky (my breath!) and all that blue—*
>
> *Lapis, and Sèvres, and borage—every hue*
> *Of blue-jay—indigo bunting—bluebird's flight.*

There are three lines underneath, with a circle drawn round them and marked "another poem." They are:

31

The Indigo Bunting

I will control myself, or go inside.
I will not flaw perfection with my grief.
Handsome, this day: no matter who has died.

2

The Sea Gull

DURING the summer of 1945, at the end of the war, we lived in a cottage by the sea, near Tenants Harbor on the coast of Maine. This is on the peninsula below Rockland, looking out on Penobscot Bay and the various islands (North Haven, South Haven, and the rest). I am a Vermonter by elective affinity, but my wife, who was brought up on the south coast of England and lulled to sleep throughout her childhood by the sound of the waves and the foghorns and the loud cries of ships, had very much the same feeling as Edna Millay about the necessity from time to time of living near sea water. Toward the end of that summer our friend Esther Adams, who has the same unfortunate predilections and spends all the time she can in her own house on the coast, asked us to come down there for a week end: the Boissevains would be there, on their way out to their own island. Esther lives at the far end of Bailey's Island, which escapes being a peninsula only by three bridges—a civilized island indeed—but nevertheless it is Maine, smelling of lobster and seaweed, and frequently so invaded by the mists of the sea that you cannot tell your hand from your mitten except by experiment.

We drove down to Bailey's Island on a bright day and only began to dive into the ocean fog as we came near to Esther's house. The Boissevains had not arrived yet, and Esther showed us over the house with her usual enthusiasm, emphasizing the beauty of the various views which were now quite shrouded in mist. We laughed at her exuberance, as we always do, and she told us that once upon a time a friend had come to stay there, remained three whole days, and on departing asked her if the ocean was visible from her house. Since she lives practically in it, with sea water on three sides of her, it may be seen that the fog on that occasion was of the first category. The one we had on our week end was of the second or third: it came and went, and we did have hours at a time of superb wind-swept clarity, sea and sun and rocks.

Toward the end of the afternoon the Boissevains arrived from Steepletop in a car loaded down with all sorts of food, pots and pans and other necessities for their stay on Ragged Island. Ragged Island, which we had just been able to discern dimly across the bay, was a pile of rocks and scrub forest, without electricity or water or communication with the mainland; it belonged to Edna and Eugen. There they went from Steepletop at intervals during the year (certainly every summer) when the desire for her native coast grew too strong for Edna to withstand. They were going to spend the night at Esther's and then go out to Ragged Island in their motor dory.

The Sea Gull

After they had extricated themselves from their accouterments we had tea in the big room where, in the evenings, there was always a fire in the vast fireplace and the wood ashes had accumulated into a mountain. Our conversation was lively, but Edna took very little part in it. She said enough to show that she was with us, although nothing more; she was rather silent and looked very frightened, small, and withdrawn. At this time she had been going through the most painful crisis any writer, and, I suppose more particularly, any poet, can experience in life, which is the inability to compose anything at all. She could not write. I had understood this and looked at her with the deepest sympathy, even though it was a time when I was still much too frightened of her to address any remark in her direction.

This requires at least a word of explanation. Miss Millay was, to put it bluntly, a frightening apparition to many of us. Her temperament was so variable that it was impossible to tell what mood might overwhelm her next; and she was obviously so painfully sensitive that any untoward phrase or sudden noise could thrust her into a private hell from which she might not emerge for days. She had been going through a bad time. I hardly knew her, and although my sympathy was profound, it was for a suffering human being whose dolor could be felt like electricity across a room: it was not for the specific person really, because I did not know that person, and it was not for the poet because at the time I had little acquaintance with her poetry. (It was not until three years later that I read it all and surrendered to it.) But most of all, I think, the reason why even the most sympathetic stranger was frightened of Edna was that she was herself so terrified. Her terror communicated itself and created terror. I hardly dared to look at her more than once or twice that evening.

Eugen, of course, knew all about this. That is probably why he was so jovial, talkative, and merry at tea and afterward, to save Edna ("Vincent" as he and all her family called her) from the pain of speech. Esther did likewise, for she, too, knew the signs. Dinah, who had known and loved Edna's poetry since schooldays, was a little abashed and concerned over the presence (and silence) of an idol. Thus we were rather a strained and uneasy company, with two carrying the burden for all.

And Edna herself, whom I have previously described as an astonishing beauty on occasion, had the capacity at such times to become so small and mouselike that one imagined she might actually vanish at any moment. Her green eyes departed; her hair was still and not red; her body grew smaller; she was for the most part away. The effect I am suggesting must have been familiar to many people, for I have heard similar things said of her.

We walked out on the terrace, since the fog had providentially lifted, and tried to see Ragged Island across the bay in the twilight. Then something happened, I do not know quite what: Eugen probably went to see about the luggage and Esther and Dinah to see about dinner; I was left on the terrace with Edna. It was rapidly getting darker and she was so shadowy and small that I could not discern her features. She sat on the wooden wall which surrounded the octagonal terrace and I took my place (rather uneasily) not far away. The side she was sitting on was the one which faced east, toward her own island. The wall had hardy rose bushes (the Rosa rugosa) underneath it and a sudden slope beyond which was the brief beach and the sea. We were silent for a long time while she looked out to sea. Then she said, in her deep voice, not quite the deepest but deep, "Thank you for the roses. They lasted a long time."

If my life had depended upon it I could not have said one word. I had sent her no roses. What could she mean? Was she confusing me with somebody else? No: she had known me clearly. Could it be that Dinah had sent her roses? Or had Esther done so and kindly put my name in with them? There had been no roses in the car, and none brought in when the Boissevains came in. My mind was whirling with suppositions. Perhaps it was a poetic way of saying something quite different. I did not know; I felt that I probably would never understand anything anyhow. The silence went on and on. She continued to look out to sea. It continued to grow darker and the fog closed in. Then suddenly a bird in the Rosa rugosa just underneath the wall where we sat began to sing loudly, merrily, on three or four notes, repeating it I think about twice.

"What's that?" I asked, startled into utterance. "What does he say?"

"That is the —" she said in her most composed, grave tone, like a teacher, naming the bird (which I have forgotten). "He lives in Maryland, usually on the Eastern Shore. He is on his way north. Perhaps he is going to Nova Scotia. He says that this is a nice place, that the evening is calm, and that he believes he will rest here for the night before going on."

"How do you know?"

"I have listened to him for a long time," she said gravely. "I have listened to them all for a long time."

I remember all of this, practically speaking word by word, except the name of that bird—to which I shall be grateful forever even though he must be for me anonymous. But for him that silence might have been eternal.

Esther then came out and told us we must get ready for dinner and we went in.

When I got upstairs I asked Dinah if she had sent roses to Miss Millay.

"Certainly not," she said. "What's the matter?"

I told her and asked if she believed Esther might have done so.

"If Esther sent roses she wouldn't put your name on them," Dinah said with great good sense. "Don't invent complications. It must be something else."

The Boissevains were off in the morning before I got up, leaving word that we were all to come to Ragged Island some day soon.

We spent that day roaming on Bailey's Island in intermittent sunshine, clambering part of the time near the sea among what seemed to me "anfractuous rocks," in T. S. Eliot's phrase. I had not yet seen Ragged Island, where the rocks were even more anfractuous. We went to the lobstermen's pier and we went down to see the boat come in from Boston and Portland; we had two meals which consisted, as I remember, largely of lobster (so did most of our meals that summer, since meat was almost unobtainable, but we never grew tired of lobster).

It was almost two months later when we did actually visit Ragged Island for the first and only time. Esther Adams herself, who could see it distinctly from her house, and through whose good offices the island had come into Edna's possession, had never visited it for the first twelve years after the Boissevains bought it. It was a place of retreat entirely, and there was an elaborate system of signals established—a big white sheet, as I remember—to indicate whether it was all right for us to come on out one day in September.

In the morning we met Eugen at the pier where his boat was tied up. He had accumulated a load of provisions and supplies of all sorts, including kerosene and gasoline, for their desert island, having come over early in the morning for that purpose. He was hearty and happy as ever, the great hulk of a man, hauling at ropes and heaving ho like a mariner born. To me, as wary of boats as of the mother tigress, it was encouraging to see how gleefully he treated the perils of the sea. The boat looked as if it might capsize at any moment, either from overloading or from leaks or from the general gusty robustiousness of the Atlantic morning. However, as we got out into deep water and began to fall into a sort of rhythm of movement, and the whole rocky coast stood up in dramatic outline, the sheer pleasure of a clear morning (for there was no mist out here) and a brisk wind dispelled whatever uneasiness I felt. It took us about forty-five minutes to get out to the island; the motor dory was perhaps not as powerful as its wheezy noise might have indicated. At last we headed toward a small pile of rocks: this was Ragged Island. And as we turned into the inlet, just as Eugen shut off the motor to go coasting in, Edna appeared at the top of the path and came swiftly down through the rocks, half running.

It was then that I saw one of the characteristic and inexplicable things associated with her personality for me. There were circling round and round her head all the way down through the rocks, three sea gulls. She came toward us, as you might say, in a completely legendary manner, down through the anfractuous rocks, left and right and then straight forward, waving her arms at us, and in spite of all this movement (and especially the arm movement, which should have been most alarming to them) the sea gulls kept her company all the way, circling round and round. She had to jump from rock to rock in the last bit, over purling rivulets of sea water, until she reached the big flat stones which formed the little quadrangular port. Here the sea gulls, seeing her safe at her destination, or espying strangers, took off into the blue with a few sad squawks. I asked both Dinah and Esther if they had seen all this; they had. And even though I have such unimpeachable fellow witnesses it still seems to me passing strange.

This legend of the rocks, when we saw her close up, was dressed in blue jeans and a white sports shirt. The jeans were rolled up almost to the knee and she had canvas sandals of some kind on her feet. She was glowing with health and spirits; her red hair was blown free and her green eyes were shining. She was in every respect different from the mouselike stranger of two months before. She hauled at ropes and asked Eugen lively questions ("Did you get this? Did you get that? Did you remember the thingumbob and I hope you didn't forget the tiddlywinks?") meanwhile greeting the rest of us with the sudden decorum, half schoolgirl and half teacher, which was her manner with most of her acquaintances. Then she and Eugen loaded all the provisions into a wheelbarrow which had been stationed at the foot of the path to receive them, and while he went back to make the boat really fast against a change in the tide, she suddenly turned to the wheelbarrow and whisked up the path so fast that she was about a third of the way up before we knew what she was doing.

"Hey, hey!" I yelled, chasing after her. "Don't do that! Let me do it!"

She went so fast that I was alarmed; we had heard stories of illness, a collapse—there were such stories periodically—and I did not think she could be strong enough to do what she was doing. She had not looked so strong before.

She glanced over her shoulder.

"Nonsense," she said indifferently, never slackening her pace. "I do this all the time. I'm used to it."

I doubt very much if I could have done it, anyhow at such speed.

The others were far behind us; I kept close to Edna, a trifle breathlessly, because of the aforesaid stories about her recent illness. She drew up at the door of the cottage with a triumphant snort.

"Ha!" she said, throwing her right hand out in a gesture, on the whole very rare with her. "You see? You didn't think I could do it. Now go to work and help me unload the things."

We unloaded the wheelbarrow and set the provisions out on the kitchen table; presently the others came.

The house was bare indeed, a few chairs and tables, some books, two or three beds. It was on the windswept top of the hill, with the forested part of the island behind it and all the bare sweep and slope and the rocky promontories in front of it. The Boissevains wanted and needed very little here; during the weeks they spent on the island in summer they were for the most part asleep during hours of darkness and awake during hours of light. Edna spent long periods at a time in the water; she was part mermaid, apparently, and was quite insensible to cold or to fatigue in water; she always swam naked, and her love for the sea was as simple and direct as the love of the lark for the sky. Eugen was less thoroughly a sea child and during her incredible durations in the water he would be setting lobster pots or bringing in the lobsters, cleaning up the house or repairing nets for fishing.

There was a great iron pot outside the kitchen, in the open air, and after we had sat for a few minutes over a drink (brought out by us—they had none on the island then) a roaring wood fire was built under it and water poured into the pot. This was for the lobsters, which at the moment sprawled in a wooden box. When she thought it was time, it was Edna who tossed the lobsters into the pot, tended the fire and watched over the cooking. It was the only time I ever saw her do any cooking (if that is cooking). While the others talked and laughed over their drinks inside, I watched her poke at the fire and stare thoughtfully at the pot. We fell to talking of work, of writing, and she said (what I already knew) that she was in difficulty.

"I haven't been able to write anything at all for a long time," she said plainly and sadly—a simple declarative sentence which for any writer is heavy to say. "It sometimes seems to me that it is all over—that it will never come again."

"If you changed to something quite different it might release you in some way," I suggested tentatively. "There might be some tension that would go. Prose."

"Prose is difficult," she said.

"The prose of poets is very special," I said. "Sometimes it is more beautiful than any other prose. Anyhow it is more exact. It selects with more precision."

"It isn't for me," she said slowly, as if thinking aloud. "I'm afraid of it. And yet, the fact is that I have often wanted to write something about Gerard Hopkins. A whole book perhaps. I have wanted to do it for a long time, merely to explain certain things which I feel to be true and which need explaining."

A book about Father Hopkins had come out not long before (in the preceding year, I believe); it was by a lady named Eleanor Ruggles and I had recently read it. I asked Edna if she had seen it.

"Yes," she said, "I read it and I was interested. But that's about his personality and his life, and chiefly about his religion. I'm not primarily interested in his Catholicism, which is what most of these books are about. His personality, his life experiences, his Catholicism, his priesthood—all those are causes. I have wanted to write about his poetry itself. It does not seem to me to have been understood."

"You mean technically?"

"Perhaps I do mean technically. I'm not sure. There are meanings that have been obscured or changed. I think it's the meaning

43

that I have in mind, but of course it can't be separated: it's all the same thing really."

Among the unwritten books I know of, this one of Edna's about the poetry of Hopkins is one of those most to be regretted.

Presently the company was reunited and decided that the meal should be taken down and eaten on the rocks. There were also bread and cheese and wine besides the lobsters, and the whole repast was stowed away in two baskets which Eugen and I carried. We went down by another way—not toward the tiny harbor, but eastward over the broad slope toward the farthest promontory. The sun had now come out in considerable brilliance and it was almost warm. Eugen and I took our shirts off when we got down there. The rocks had turned a warmer brown in the sun and when we really got to our place, all rocks indeed, a prong sticking out into the sea, the heat of the sun was thrown back at us with almost midsummer vigor.

The meal was wonderfully good and there was the kind of laughter which depends more on good spirits, good company, and well-being than upon any particular *trouvaille* of humor. We had dishes and cutlery and glasses, all in fine style, which was just as convenient on these clean rocks, with all their washed flat spaces, as in any dining room. I remember thinking how different this was, in the fringe of the scented sea, from those country picnics in which everything seems to spill into everything else, there is no level surface and above all no difference of levels, and only the ants and the flies appear to enjoy their meal. Here we could eat from any one of a score of tables of any height we chose, all swept and garnished by the good strong tides in the livery of our lady the moon. We scattered ourselves at various heights and in various interstices, with the sea lapping in and out here and there among the rocks. The smell of the sea was of the pure, clear kind, because deep water began immediately there and there was no seaweed or death-débris as on a shore to make it heavy and sour. We looked about for some old bits of dry wood to make a fire when we had eaten, and on the fire Eugen set the coffeepot to boil. As we sat there, Edna, who was sitting on a flat rock at the top of our central space, threw back her head and looked out to sea and began to say verses. I had never heard her do so before. Her incomparable voice seemed to be thrown out at the sea, not loudly at all but directly, full and deep as the salt water. The verses she said were her penultimate sonnet in *Epitaph for the Race of Man*: it is the one which begins

> *Only the diamond and the diamond's dust*
> *Can render up the diamond unto Man.*

The verses are abstract and rather brittle, but at the time the full glory and astonishment of her voice in poetry quite obliterated everything else; I hardly understood a word she said because the sound itself was so beautiful. This sonnet had some special recondite meaning, some association from the past, for Edna and Esther, which was how it was called forth. But once she had said those lines we were unable to let her subside; we begged for more and she said some more. I do not know precisely which of her poems she said to us, but I like to think that this might have been one:

The Indigo Bunting

People that build their houses inland,
    People that buy a plot of ground
Shaped like a house, and build a house there,
    Far from the sea-board, far from the sound

Of water sucking the hollow ledges,
    Tons of water striking the shore,—
What do they long for, as I long for
    One salt smell of the sea once more?

People the waves have not awakened,
    Spanking the boats at the harbour's head,
What do they long for, as I long for,—
    Starting up in my inland bed,

Beating the narrow walls, and finding
    Neither a window nor a door,
Screaming to God for death by drowning,—
    One salt taste of the sea once more?

And then it might have been this:

Searching my heart for its true sorrow,
    This is the thing I find to be:
That I am weary of words and people,
    Sick of the city, wanting the sea;

Wanting the sticky, salty sweetness
    Of the strong wind and shattered spray;
Wanting the loud sound and the soft sound
    Of the big surf that breaks all day.

Always before about my dooryard,
    Marking the reach of the winter sea,

The Sea Gull

Rooted in sand and dragging drift-wood,
 Straggled the purple wild sweet-pea;

Always I climbed the wave at morning,
 Shook the sand from my shoes at night,
That now am caught beneath great buildings,
 Stricken with noise, confused with light.

If I could hear the green piles groaning
 Under the windy wooden piers,
See once again the bobbing barrels,
 And the black sticks that fence the weirs,

If I could see the weedy mussels
 Crusting the wrecked and rotting hulls,
Hear once again the hungry crying
 Overhead, of the wheeling gulls,

Feel once again the shanty straining
 Under the turning of the tide,
Fear once again the rising freshet,
 Dread the bell in the fog outside,

I should be happy!—that was happy
 All day long on the coast of Maine;
I have a need to hold and handle
 Shells and anchors and ships again!

I should be happy . . . that am happy
 Never at all since I came here.
I am too long away from water.
 I have a need of water near.

We threw lobster shells into the wet rocks where the tide would suck them away, and everytime a shell went out there was a swoop of sea gulls over it. Dinah remembers that the sky was inky-blue, of the color called indigo—not at all the color of the indigo bunting, but dark dark dark—with white frills around the brown rocks of the island. At one point, I remember, after we had finished our coffee, she told Edna about a passage I had written in the book upon which I was then engaged. This book (which was called *This House Against This House*) had to do with the closing phases of the war and the opening phases of the "peace." It contained about eight to ten pages about India, which I had visited only as an army officer on a specific job of work (the B-29 operation) in 1944. I was later to visit India more than once, and in a very different manner, but even that first visit made me extremely uneasy with the perception of something I tried to define in the book as a new kind of force, a "mass-and-nature co-conscious reality" arising out of the combination of material misery and deep philosophical tradition. In that passage I remarked that even the most thoughtless soldier seemed to feel this in India (even if only at the sight of a snake charmer or a village *yogi*) and to resent it bitterly as being strange, unfamiliar, unknown.

My wife, quoting something from this passage which had puzzled her, asked Edna Millay if she had felt anything of the sort in India.

"I did," said Edna positively. "I was aware of it the moment I stepped off the boat. It may be the numbers. Many and one, or one and many—they seem to be the same. And there is some sense of mystery in ordinary life, too, which is stronger there than anywhere else. I can't say what it is, exactly, but there is something there that doesn't exist in our life at all, and doesn't exist in Chinese life either. I can't explain it, but I do know that it is true. The resentment of the unfamiliar is also true, but in my case it didn't last long."

She said other things on that subject but I am unable to remember them clearly enough to make an intelligible paraphrase. The gist was that she had experienced very much what I had on first acquaintance with that immense and teeming country. My wife, who had then never been in India, was at a loss to guess what this inexplicable extra consciousness was; some years later she was to go to India and find out.

After we had sufficiently enticed and encouraged the sea gulls with lobster shells, we packed up our two baskets and set off up the slope again to the cottage. Here Edna had a brief nap while Eugen cleaned up the débris. Esther, Dinah, and I took a walk to the other side of the island, which was entirely different, all forested and above a declivity with no rocks. As we made our way through the woods, lovely with the sun through the green even though they were still a trifle dank, I asked Esther what was the meaning of a phrase I had heard Edna say to Eugen: "Mrs. Jones is dead." Esther said she thought there were two crippled sea gulls, known as Mrs. Jones and Mrs. Smith, whom Edna had been feeding for two days, and that one of these had evidently died.

"The wind beats them against the rocks and they break a leg or a wing," Esther explained. "Then Edna tries to take care of them. She usually succeeds."

When we got back to the cottage Edna and Eugen declared

that it was time to bathe. Life was to a very considerable extent regulated by the tides on Ragged Island: it was best to bathe near high tide when the little harbor was full of calm, clear water—that is, unless you wished to entrust yourself to the rough open sea. It was best to take the boat out or in, set lobster pots or haul them, in accordance with the tides, which accordingly came to assume the importance which clocks have usurped in more terrestrial abodes.

We all trailed down the path to the little harbor and the sea gulls did make one or two attempts to fly over Edna again, I thought; at least they came, but they soon went. We were too many for them. I was reminded of Mrs. Jones and Mrs. Smith, and enquired.

"She had a badly broken leg and no doubt some internal injuries," Edna explained. "She must have been hurled against the rocks with great force. The other one is doing well and is really quite tame now. They acknowledge the necessity when they are crippled. They're very free birds, you know, not at all tameable."

I asked her how she explained the behavior of the three gulls who had circled round her head as she came down the path this morning. From her answer I could not be sure that she had been conscious of them—or, being conscious, would venture an opinion on their behavior.

"Oh, they know me, I suppose, a little bit," she said. "I'm here so much. I don't know."

She went on a bit, abstracted, and then said the inevitable: "And then, too, I feed them."

"But so did we all!" I protested. "You don't see any gulls circling round my head, do you?"

She laughed and refused to pursue this any further.

"Nobody ever wears a bathing suit at Ragged Island," she said
decisively when we had arrived at the harbor. "It's a rule of the
island. We think bathing dress of any sort is indecent, and so do
the waves and so do the sea gulls and so does the wind. No bathing dress has been seen on Ragged Island since we came here."

This sounded authoritative, and the two visitors (Esther and
I) who had brought some sort of gear for swimming put it down
on the rocks rather apologetically. Esther vanished into her
favorite pool among the rocks; Dinah did not bathe at all and had
never intended to anyhow; Eugen and Edna and I stripped on
the flat rocks by the port and went into the water.

I had never bathed naked in the sea before and was astonished
at the difference it made in the feeling of the water. Edna, who
was to all intents and purposes a sea creature, treated the salt
water as an element as native as air: sometimes she swam vigor-
ously, sometimes she floated, sometimes she seemed merely to lie
in the water without any sort of movement, even that required
for floating. How she did it I do not know. She would do this for
a whole morning at a time, and had always been impervious to
any sort of cramp or cold or fatigue in water. She had been born
on the Maine Coast—at Rockland, near where we were living
that summer—and had grown up at Camden, the beautiful
little town a little north of Rockland: this was her country and
her ocean. I am a very poor swimmer, hardly a swimmer at all,

and kept to my depth, but Edna and to a lesser degree Eugen treated the whole stretch of nearby waters as their bailiwick.

Eugen, once he had removed his blue toweling shirt and his dungarees, revealed a powerful body which was mahogany in color from the sun—mahogany all over. Edna absorbed the sun in quite a different way from Eugen—not the deep red-brown of a leather-cured skin, but a softer nut-brown color which looked as if it were not from the skin alone but went on inward. Emerging from the sea at last, dripping and with green eyes ashine, she looked as if she had regained some particular strength from the long immersion. By the time she came out we had—the rest of us—long been sunning ourselves on the great flat rock, where the refraction made the day seem a great deal warmer than it actually was.

When we went back up to the cottage there occurred a little incident which, I have always thought, established some form of communication between Edna and me in spite of our extremely limited acquaintance—an acquaintance which was never to be extensive in the sense of time or frequency, but only, I think, in depth. I had a flat, thin watch which I had bought in Geneva a good ten years before; it is known in our family as "the Geneva watch," and whenever it sustains an accident and must be repaired the length of time it takes to get it done seems endless, the money involved exorbitant. I value it perhaps in part because of these difficulties, and have it still, although I am a great loser of all other objects.

We were in the kitchen of the cottage, having a drink and talking about supper and the journey over to Bailey's Island—

52

whether to have supper here and then go or go first and eat at Esther's. The question was settled, as usual, by the tide, and we were to have supper here. Sometime during this discussion I crossed the floor of the kitchen toward the table where the drinks were and my Geneva watch, insecurely fastened or forgotten after the swim, fell out and crashed on the floor. I knelt to pick it up, saying by habit: "Christ Jesus Our Lord and Him Crucified!"

I heard Edna behind me say softly: "Between two thieves."

When I got up with the watch in my hand I looked at her and she looked at me. This was, I believe, the first time we had ever looked directly at each other. I think we were friends from then on, and would have been anyhow whether I had ever seen her again or not.

The mainspring of the watch was broken and it cost a good deal to have it repaired, incidentally. But it was well worth it.

During this placid interval before we busied ourselves with supper Esther was moved to speak of Edna's poems for children. At this time I knew hardly anything about Edna's poetry; I never had known that she wrote poems for children or about children. Something "Tess" said set her off. She cocked her head on one side, put her feet apart and suddenly looked about twelve years old. She said:

> *Look, Edwin! Do you see that boy*
> *Talking to the other boy?*
> *No, over there by those two men—*
> *Wait, don't look now—now look again.*
> *No, not the one in navy-blue;*

The Indigo Bunting

That's the one he's talking to.
Sure you see him? Stripèd pants?
Well, he was born in Paris, France.

And she said:

Come along in then, little girl!
Or else stay out!
But in the open door she stands,
And bites her lip and twists her hands,
And stares upon me, trouble-eyed:
"Mother," she says, "I can't decide!
I can't decide!"

The command which Edna Millay had over the mood of her own verses and the projection of that mood must be well known; after all, she made several tours of the United States talking about her poems and reading them. But I had never seen or heard her do it until this day, and it was startling to me. I am, in fact, impervious to the reading of poetry in any set manner, in any way which suggests the stage or dramatic interpretation or other visible or audible enactment. But what Edna Millay did was not "dramatic reading" or, in any precise sense, acting. It was the projection of a mood by the simplest of means. There she stood (in the one about Paris, France) with her feet apart and her head on one side, nothing else: she was a woman turned fifty, dressed in rolled-up dungarees and a white sports shirt, and nevertheless she looked like a little girl of twelve at a party. And in the second, merely by putting her feet and hands together, and by a cooler color in her voice, she became the little girl who could not decide. Both were vivid, each was different, and both were as unlike the sea poems at noon on the rocks as it is possible to imagine. She unquestionably had a particular talent for this kind of expression, whatever it may be called. I have never seen or heard a similar phenomenon, in which the words, voice, and body all became parts of the specific single mood (so brief, too!) which she wished to transmit. It was a form of being, not of doing.

We supped in the kitchen, also on lobster—cold by now—and some of the wine was left to drink with it. Edna did not touch drinks or wine that day: she had, in fact, been extremely ill, although her exploits with the wheelbarrow had seemed to deny it. Her look of glowing health was (so Eugen told us) highly deceptive, and came largely from her joy at being on her beloved island again. We talked a good deal about Maine that evening, and about Rockland, where she was born and where my wife's mother and aunt had been born; and about Camden, where Edna had spent her girlhood before she went to Vassar; and about the lake not far from Camden where friends of ours were living that summer. It was odd that anybody like Edna, I was thinking, should have come from Rockland, which, although a fine town and a good port in the old days or even now, is hardly what you would pick as a cradle for poets. And yet was it any odder than the fact that my wife's mother and aunt, Gertrude and Maxine Elliott, whose lives had taken them very much into another world, should have been born there? We had recently been to see the little house where they were born, upon which the State Woman's Club of Maine had put up a bronze plaque. You could have put the whole house into one end of the big drawing room of Maxine's "Chateau de l'Horizon" in the south of France, where the end of her life was passed. We told Edna about this and it made her laugh. I suppose there must be a bronze plaque on the house where she was born by now, if it is still standing; and no doubt it is or was just as small as the other, for the Millays were poor too. America.

We had to go.

The sea had been indigo-blue all day and was darker still now in the burnished light of a sun about to set. Edna came down to the boat with us and was extremely efficient about nautical arrangements. Something was lost, I forget what, and Esther found it.

"How," she demanded in her pride, "does anybody live without me?"

Edna spoke very drily, savoring her little joke. "The question is," she said, "do they?"

We left the little port in a roar of noise from the indignant motor and Edna stood there waving until we could see her no more. The journey back was beautiful in the agitated dark sea with the sky in a turmoil of vanishing lights and colors. Presently it was colder and darker and the mist rose softly from the sea, softly and wetly, so that we were glad to get out of the boat at Bailey's Island; Eugen turned round at once to go back. The *Greasy Joan*—that was the boat—could make no speed quick enough to get him back to Edna.

I remembered about the roses. It had been coming back in shreds all day long—something from years before. There had been an occasion, and at first I could not for the life of me remember which, when somebody had sent flowers in my name to Edna St. Vincent Millay (whom I knew even less then). It was some curious occasion not to be fully realized or understood in connection with her: something rather impersonal or official or public in nature, something that had to do with crowds and ceremonies and speeches. It came back in that way, small and incongruous patches fitting together not at all. I remembered Wendell Willkie and his broad, warm grin that could never be forgotten—that was part of it—and something about feathered and flowered hats.

Hats! That did it.

In the year 1940, toward the end of the year, well after the presidential elections were over, the United China Relief was formed out of seven existing bodies which had previously been attempting (at cross-purposes and competitively in some degree) to get money to help sufferers in the Chinese war of resistance to Japan. The leading spirit in this unification of effort was Henry Luce, who with characteristic energy welded all the worthy committees into one, added a good many public figures to the letterhead, and engaged in a campaign to collect ten million dollars. (At the time I thought it far too much; but we collected more than that.) For some reason Mr. Luce wanted me to be chairman of the first big dinner, at the Waldorf, to launch the new organization and the new campaign. I had been chairman of a writers' committee on one of the component organizations and Mr. Luce decided that the opening gun was to be fired as from this committee, with me introducing the notables. These included Wendell Willkie, Pearl Buck, both the Luces, and some others (Mr. Paul Hoffman also—he afterward became chairman of United China Relief). A number of writers were invited to sit at the speaker's table, and Miss Edna St. Vincent Millay was asked to say a poem.

To operate all this efficiently, Mr. Luce engaged a lady whose business it was to engineer and conduct such large drives for funds. This is, it seems, a profession, and she was a seasoned professional in that business. She was a woman of charm and humor, and her methods were my delight for some weeks. She thought nothing of telephoning to some tremendous dignitary, such as (for example) Mr. Rockefeller, and asking for any form of moral or financial support—usually in my name: a thing I could never have done myself. She had little secret-service reports (mimeographed) on which celebrated person was staying in which hotel in New York, and who had gone and who had come. She had a passion for getting photographs taken, on the theory that these would somehow get into newspapers and would somehow elicit dollars for China from some hiding place. Thus we were all photographed innumerable times—all those involved in the new enterprise—and my wife has to this day an album which contains a vast collection of pictures taken of Clare Luce, Wendell, Pearl Buck, and others, with my unphotogenic countenance in their midst. It was a strange episode to me, but it apparently worked and apparently that is how such things are done.

Now, this lady who managed everything wore a different hat each day. It was her mania and it added much gayety to the office of China Relief. Plumes and feathers, feathers and plumes, ribbons and glitters, sprays and lace—every conceivable variety of head adornment was hers. I never thought of her without one of these fantasies on her head. The moment I remembered hats I knew all about the roses.

Edna Millay had come to the dinner in her smallest and most frightened mood. She had been very ill and she had worried immeasurably over Hitler's victories in Europe and the disappearance of so many brave small countries, including Eugen's. The atmosphere at the Waldorf was not favorable to her. When I saw her come into the sitting room where the speakers gathered I thought she looked like a stricken deer and I tried to take care of her. There was much to do, but the lady with the hats was doing most of it, and I spent ten or fifteen minutes with Edna.

Then we marched into the big ballroom, marshaled by the lady of the hats, and took our places at a long table. The glare of the lights (the bluish lights used when photographs are constantly being taken) was frightful. I wondered how Edna would stand it and looked down the table. There she was, looking more woebegone than words can say, refusing to sit down—standing behind her chair. I went behind all the notables and got to her and asked what was the matter.

"I can't sit with strangers only," she said in an agonized whisper. "Please, I must have Eugen sitting beside me. Believe me, it's true. I don't know what will happen if he isn't here. Please, please—otherwise I'll have to go home."

I could see that she did not exaggerate in the slightest. She was trembling all over. I went at once to Pearl Buck, since the lady of the hats was not visible, and told her that Miss Millay was not well and must have her husband with her. Pearl understood at once and did some extremely rapid and efficient business with the headwaiter or somebody, so that Eugen was placed beside Edna.

At this time I had no idea that Edna had been asked to recite a poem. I simply went through the program as it was given to me by the lady with the hats, introducing the speakers in a given order with as much brevity as the law allows. Some of the program was broadcast and when Wendell Willkie spoke it suddenly went on one or two of the national networks. I plowed through it as best I could, sweating profusely from those abominable blue lights, and at the end of the whole proceeding Dinah and I escaped as rapidly as possible. We did not see Edna or Eugen during our flight.

On the following morning I went to the office of United China Relief, by request, to receive reports from the lady with the hats. She then told me that Edna had been supposed to read a poem and that there had been no time for it: it had been squeezed out by all the speeches of the public notables, which had to be timed precisely because of the radio broadcasting.

I was horrified and also shocked. Nobody at that dinner had said anything worth remembering. It was a writers' dinner, and I was chairman of it, and yet there was no room for a poem by Edna Millay! It seemed to me such a characteristic piece of New Yorkism, in which only the inflated, the evanescent, and the forgettable has any value, that I expressed myself in decided language.

"I was about to suggest," said the lady with the hats, "that you write a note of regret to Miss Millay and I will send it to her with some flowers."

"But I hardly know Miss Millay," I said. "And moreover I can't imagine what to say to her. It's such a stupid outrage."

"Say whatever you like," said the hat lady, "and I'll get the flowers and send them. I know where she is staying."

She added with a demure smile: "China Relief can afford it this morning. We did very well last night."

I wrote something—I have no idea what—to Edna, and gave it to the lady.

"What flowers will you send?" I asked.

"Whatever's nicest," she said. "I think perhaps I'll send roses."

So that was that!

Five years had passed and still she remembered the roses. "They lasted a long time."

There had been a moment down on the rocks this day when Edna had talked more or less directly to me about China, which she loved (as I do) and in which she had felt, on that same world journey with Eugen, the power and omnipresence of design—of a world with a pattern clearer perhaps to us because we do not belong to it, but clear just the same. It was a moment in that city of the rocks when the others had wandered or were busy; in any case we did talk about China more or less alone. She told me about the boatman she remembered so well—Pao-Chin, his name—on a day when she and Eugen went out on the Yellow Sea, and of his self-possession and decorum. I told her about my only journey over the Yellow Sea, which was on a bombing raid against a Japanese munitions plant in Manchuria. She said her view of that body of water had been different. She had written verses to Pao-Chin. And she said:

> *Where is he now, in his soiled shirt reeking of garlic,*
> *Sculling his sampan home, and night approaching fast—*
> *The red sail hanging wrinkled on the bamboo mast;*
> *Where is he now, I shall remember my whole life long*
> *With love and praise, for the sake of a small song*
> *Played on a Chinese flute?*
> > *I have been sad;*
> *I have been in cities where the song was all I had,—*
> *A treasure never to be bartered by the hungry days.*
>
> *Where is he now, for whom I carry in my heart*
> *This love, this praise?*

We went back to Esther's house on Bailey's Island and sat by the fire and talked a good deal about Edna. At that time, as I have already said, I knew scarcely anything about her poetry. If I were today to characterize at least some of my feeling about that day in verses written by her, I should choose "The Bobolink." It goes:

Black bird scudding
Under the rainy sky,
How wet your wings must be!
And your small head how sleek and cold with water.

Oh, Bobolink, 'tis you!
Over the buffeted orchard in the summer draught,
Chuckling and singing, charging the rainy cloud,

The Sea Gull

A little bird gone daft,
A little bird with a secret.

Only the bobolink on the rainy
Rhubarb blossom,
Knows my heart . . .
For whom adversity has not a word to say that can be heard
Above the din of summer.
The rain has taught us nothing. And the hooves of cattle, and the
  cat in the grass
Have taught us nothing.

The hawk that motionless above the hill
In the pure sky
Stands like a blackened planet
Has taught us nothing,—seeing him shut his wings and fall
Has taught us nothing at all.
In the shadow of the hawk we feather our nests.

Bobolink, you and I, an airy fool and an earthy,
Chuckling under the rain!

I shall never be sad again.
I shall never be sad again.

Ah, sweet, absurd,
Belovèd, bedraggled bird!

When it came time to pack to go home I observed that the shirt I had worn at Ragged Island was no longer with us. I had gone without a shirt all day and all the way home, and had simply forgotten it. It was a shirt from a shop entitled "Adao"—pronounced Adamo and meaning Adam, if my Portuguese does not fail me—in Lisbon, and had no particular economic or

63

aesthetic value. I merely assumed that it would serve as a cleaning rag sometime and forgot it. Three years later at Steepletop Edna returned it to me, beautifully washed and ironed (she said by herself). The Lisbon shirt is still with me, and I never see it without thinking of her extraordinary memory, her odd decorum, her gratitude for the roses.

But the chief pith and marrow of the day at Ragged Island, after all, came at the beginning. It is that I shall remember until the light fades for ever: Edna coming like a legend down through the anfractuous rocks with three sea gulls circling round her head.

3

The Birds

"BIRDS fly all through her poetry," says Norma Millay, and those who have read Edna's books know that it is true. I have already confessed my own belated acquaintance with this exquisite work to which I came only after I had had some glimpses of its creator. There is little profit or pleasure in "evaluating" it—even if I could—or in comparing it to anything else. For the purposes of this essay it is enough to say that I, like many others, find in it a singing line, a contained and articulated melody, quite unlike other verse of its (or our) time. It sings, like the indigo bunting, "in late summer when other bird voices are still."

And although its predominant theme from first to last is love, woman's love, its constant appeal to the forces of surrounding nature, above all to the sea and to the birds, is what gives it a haunting peculiarity in modern poetry. This appeal to the natural environment for every ratification of emotion, every beat of the wing, was far more common in the great ages of poetry

The Indigo Bunting

(Elizabethan or Romantic) than it is in the metaphysical stage to which the art has now progressed. And if I have been able to convey anything of Edna's quality as a person, it may be seen that this appeal to the natural environment was as inevitable as breathing for her: she was far more at home with the sea and the birds, far more in communication, than she ever was with human beings so far as I know.

This would seem to be in contradiction to the testimony of so much of her own poetry, which celebrates the joys and aftermaths of human physical love as explicitly as they have ever been celebrated. But that, as I have ventured to say, is the theme, and not a new one: it is in the reference to that larger life within which human life is contained that Edna's verse takes on extra dimensions, enlarges its own deceptive simplicities and relates to a concept which she never fully admitted but which, as a sort of rock-bottom idiosyncratic pantheism, coloring her existence and determining her behavior, will be seen in time to have set her poems apart and helped give them the grace to be remembered.

Her very first poem, written (or rather made up) at the age of five or six, was about birds; and so was the last fragment we have quoted. Through the intervening years the appeal to these creatures as a sort of kindred is almost incessant. It is least marked in *Renascence,* the first volume, and then grows in a crescendo through *Second April, The Harp Weaver,* and the succeeding volumes until it is cut short by a deep concern over the state of human society toward the end of the 1930's. This phase, which produced poems about Spain and Czechoslovakia, was misunderstood at the time, but was as natural and inevitable in Edna Millay's development as any other.

The poems actually written about specific birds are not very numerous. The bobolink, the wild swan, the pigeons, English sparrows, and the skylark have their names in the titles of lyrics; "the fledgling," of species unnamed, has a beautiful lyric to itself; one of the finest in *Huntsman, What Quarry?* is about a bird with clipped wing striving to reach the high branches; the lyrics called "Pueblo Pot" and "On Thought in Harness" are in reality about birds, as is "Short Story" and "To a Young Poet." Wren or falcon, the nature of the bird seems to breathe from the lines, and however bare they may seem in prosody they rustle with wings.

There are two sonnets, also, which are bird poems in essence. One of these concerns the nightingale (*Fatal Interview,* xx) as a symbol of indifferent beauty, indifferent love. The other (*Fatal Interview,* xlii) is of "ailing Love" conceived as a bird dying.

But these are the conscious compositions, those in which the poet sets out to write of birds because such metaphor and symbol come naturally to her. Largely they are directed upon the phenomena of human life or love, but translated into another language. How much more numerous, and, it seems, how unconscious or half-conscious, are the references to birds which strew the pages of all the other poems! Lyrics and sonnets, long or short poems, are animated by the presence of all these feathered beasts who seem to have fluttered through her imagination at all times as through a hospitable forest, supplying her with endless petitions to a reality above and beyond the limits of human experience. When I talked of this to her she denied it, or rather said that it might be so but that she was not conscious of it—the birds were so familiar to her from her earliest days that she was never aware of any particularity in her own view of them or relationship with them. The attention she gave to them seemed to her so natural, by long habit, that even this and the consequent tameness of the untameable—as witness the sea gulls—did not seem to her much out of the way. She took it for granted and refused to think about it: which, I make bold to say, proves the existence of the integument. If she had not known her good gossips and cronies so well she would have been more conscious of their incessant commerce.

Most of the birds that wing their way through her lines are American, and chiefly from the northeastern states she knew best; but from the time she spent in England, France, and Italy in the 1920's there are to be heard also the lark and the nightingale. In "The Road to Avrillé," for example:

> *The cuckoo spoke from out the wood,*
> *The lark from out the sky.*

And "West Country Song" (England):

> *Lark in air so high, and his song clean through me,*
> *Now comes night, pushing the lark in's furrow.*

Or "On First Having Heard the Skylark":

> *Not knowing he rose from earth, not having seen him rise,*
> *Not knowing the fallow furrow was his home. . . .*

The Birds

These are exceptions to the rule which makes the pigeon, sparrow, robin, sea gull, partridge, thrush, goose, cock and hen, along with all the other common creatures of the American woods, coast, and barnyard indigenous to her verse. The sonnet mentioned earlier (*Fatal Interview*, XLII) is one of those in which the bird appears simply as bird, without reference to his family. It is worth quoting in its entirety, not only as a beautiful sonnet, but as an example of the way in which Edna Millay uses the life of the bird—that is to say, the bird in general, although not in the abstract: any bird—as a projection of the life of man.

O ailing Love, compose your struggling wing!
Confess you mortal; be content to die.
How better dead, than be this awkward thing
Dragging in dust its feathers of the sky,
Hitching and rearing, plunging beak to loam,
Upturned, dishevelled, utt'ring a weak sound
Less proud than of the gull that rakes the foam,
Less kind than of the hawk that scours the ground.
While yet your awful beauty, even at bay,
Beats off the impious eye, the outstretched hand,
And what your hue or fashion none can say,
Vanish, be fled, leave me a wingless land . . .
Save where one moment down the quiet tide
Fades a white swan, with a black swan beside.

The generalization is not infrequent in her poems and is often used with an effect more startling than the specific ever could be. In "Portrait," for example (from *The Buck in the Snow*):

Beauty at such moments before me like a wild bright bird
Has been in the room, and eyed me, and let me come near it.

Or, later in the same lyric:

Rapture, coloured like the wild bird's neck and wing,
Comfort, softer than the feathers of its breast.

And, in "Intention to Escape from Him," these lines:

I think I will learn the Latin name of every songbird, not only
in America but wherever they sing.

Remains the fact, attested by the whole body of her poetry, that the simple specific bird, the rook and robin and bobolink, sparrow and pigeon, gave her by far the greatest number of images, direct and exact, arising in her own consciousness by natural processes created through her life's experience. She must, I think, from earliest childhood have felt a kinship with these creatures and no doubt longed (as many children do) to know their secret and understand their language; at any rate she is the only person I ever knew who was quite certain of the name and habit of an unseen bird by the song alone. In that sense she knew more about them than many a professorial specialist. And for good reason, for her interest never flagged and she was their devotee at the hours when they are most accessible.

The *Bird Guide,* the small, brown book so wrinkled and worn with use, the one I saw on the table at Steepletop, lies before me with its evidence of her unflagging interest during the last twelve or fifteen years of her life. No doubt there had been earlier bird guides, worn out and thrown away or lost; this one contains no notes earlier than 1934, except a rather cryptic reference to a blue jay in 1926, and to a yellow-bellied sapsucker in 1927. These might have been, it seems to me, references to some earlier experience before she possessed this little book. In any case the notes from the late 1930's and the 1940's abound. In the flyleaf are some notes about the chicken hawk, seen on April 12 of some year, with the solemn addendum that "Mr Miller of the Natural History Museum" considers the bird's name a misnomer. The mourning dove was heard on April 10, 1938, we also learn on another flyleaf.

And then, on through the book, are the dates and notes. Sometimes she saw them, sometimes she only heard them, sometimes they appeared at Steepletop and sometimes on journeys to other regions. The black-billed cuckoo, she observes on May 15, 1945, has not yet been heard at Steepletop, "perhaps because no caterpillars here." She had seen him near Spencertown, but that was near a caterpillar nest. The belted kingfisher also seems to have avoided Steepletop but was seen on the way to Stockbridge (1927) and to Austerlitz (1948). The southern downy woodpecker (a pretty carnivore by the picture) was "here all winter '49-50"—i.e., the last winter of her life, the winter after Eugen's death when she lived alone.

The flicker, nighthawk, ruby-throated hummingbird, kingbird, crested flycatcher, phoebe, wood pewee, bobolink, cowbird, red-winged blackbird, rusty blackbird, Baltimore oriole, purple grackle, evening grosbeak, pine grosbeak, purple finch, Greenland redpoll, the redpoll, American goldfinch, English sparrow, grasshopper sparrow, seaside sparrow (at Ragged Island), white-crowned sparrow, white-throated sparrow, tree sparrow, chipping sparrow, field sparrow, slate-colored junco, song sparrow, Lincoln sparrow, fox sparrow, towhee or chewink, cardinal, rose-breasted grosbeak, blue grosbeak, indigo bunting, scarlet tanager, cliff swallow (at Ragged Island), barn swallow, Bohemian waxwing, cedar waxwing, loggerhead shrike, Philadelphia vireo, yellow-throated vireo, white-eyed vireo, black and white warbler, Nashville warbler, Tennessee warbler, yellow warbler, black-throated blue warbler, myrtle warbler, magnolia warbler, cerulean warbler, chestnut-sided warbler, Blackburnian warbler, black-poll warbler, oven-bird, Kentucky warbler, Connecticut warbler, Maryland yellow-throat, Wilson warbler, Canadian warbler, American redstart, American pipit, mockingbird, catbird, brown thrasher, house wren, winter wren, brown creeper, white-breasted nuthatch, red-breasted nuthatch, black-capped chickadee, Hudsonian chickadee, golden-crowned kinglet, ruby-crowned kinglet, wood thrush, Wilson thrush, hermit thrush, American robin and bluebird are the names of the other birds in this guide to which she has penciled notes of their comings and goings, what they did and when, where they lived when they stayed at Steepletop, and sometimes a sort of lively polemical attack upon the *Bird Guide* for insufficient appreciation of their merits.

There are some ecstatic scribblings, as of the Bohemian waxwing: "Oh, at last I have seen one! (Seen two!)" Of the barn swallow, noted on April 14, 1938, she adds on April 19: "I have not seen him since, so perhaps I was mistaken. But how *could* one be mistaken about the flight of a swallow?"

The scarlet tanager "took a bath in our brook" on May 12,

1947. However, this was bourgeois conduct as compared to the kingbird (*tyrannus tyrannus*): "Every autumn they nest in orchard. I have seen one, at least, plunge into the swimming pool 6 or seven times, to bathe. Beautiful shallow dives. Got very wet, sat in cherry tree to shake & dry—several evenings, always same place."

Some of the birds noted, of course, never came near Steepletop: they were the denizens of Florida, the Grand Canyon, Santa Fé or Texas or Colorado. (The American magpie, the cardinal, and others were thus exotically beheld.) The beautiful birds of my memorable week end at Steepletop, the purple finch, rosebreasted grosbeak, and indigo bunting, all have penciled markings which fill the margins of the pages assigned to them: perhaps they were not quite so ordinary, all at once, as Edna had seemed to indicate.

It seems that on May 11, 1938, a male indigo bunting was seen "in second year plumage, very beautiful, feeding on ground outside my window, alongside a white-crowned sparrow and directly beneath a very rosy purple finch sitting on a spray of apple-blossoms." Her window sill and the ground outside her window were among her favorite places for scattering sunflower seed and other food beloved by the visitors, so it is not remarkable that so many of the notes record them there. She had "feeding stations" there and outside the living-room window as well as on the window sill of the kitchen, so that there were a number of vantage points for observation.

There are, to my surprise, some uncertainties. Of the redbreasted nuthatch: "May 26, still here, pretty sure it is this bird

—eats suet—quite tame." Of the brown creeper: "Not *sure* it was this bird." In Santa Fé on November 1 of some unnamed year she saw the Florida jay, but puts a question mark after the date and writes at the bottom of the page: "At least, it was a jay very like this—perhaps a bit darker here."

And with the *Bird Guide* itself she conducts a critical feud on a number of points, like a relative grumbling away in an undertone by the fireside. She finds too many species of birds bearing the name of "warbler," and enquires why. On the page devoted to the pine grosbeak she writes: "This is a horrible picture of a beautiful bird."

Sparrows of all kinds were her particular children, as readers of her poetry know (they must be mentioned more often than any other bird); and the *Bird Guide* was not kind enough to them. It describes the note of the English sparrow as "a harsh, discordant sound," which annoyed Edna into scribbling: "It's no such thing! It's a sweet sound, you old meanie! Just because you don't like them!"

The grasshopper sparrow has, according to the *Bird Guide*, "a weak, insect-like zee-e-e-e-e." Edna's verdict: "For some reason a thrilling little song."

There seems to be no particular reason why she chose this rather than another bird book. It has the merits of small size and adequate illustration, as well as being pretty well complete (I am told) for the part of the country in which Edna lived. It was prepared by Chester A. Reed and published first in 1906; the edition Edna used was a reissue of 1925. She did not find occasion to add much to it, except a list of the birds whose song (or notes) she knew which were not included. She observes that forty-five of the birds in the book are familiar to her by sound alone, and then scrawls in her penciled supplement.

Bird watchers say that forty-five is by no means a large number of bird species to be familiar by sound alone. To this it should be remarked that Edna undoubtedly knew double that number before she died fifteen years later, and it should also be remarked that however numerous or few her bird acquaintances, she was never in the least scientific or systematic about them—it was a poet's knowledge, not an ornithologist's.

The wrinkled brown booklet suggests the care with which she watched over the creatures, but only suggests: for the entries are erratic, often at long intervals, and always made in a very nearly illegible scrawl which shows haste and a total absence of anything like systematic study. She wanted to remember—that was all—and did in fact remember, perhaps after years of practice, better than anybody I have ever encountered. In those special hours of dawn she "stalked" the birds (her own expression in one of these notes) and learned how they nested, how they lived, what was their private song. Suet appears to have been a staple of diet for some, cornflower seed for others, but she fed them all, and the relative rarity or commonness of a bird meant little to her: we have seen that the sparrow was dearer to her than any other, if we are to judge by the frequency of his appearance in her verse.

Birds she did not know also commanded her imagination, and Robinson Jeffers has written to me that when she visited his tower at Carmel, in California—a tower by the sea which he built for himself out of stones and pebbles—she asked him many questions about hawks.

"She questioned me about the local hawks," he says, "sparrowhawk, marsh-hawk, redtail, Copper's hawk, duck hawk and so forth—but I thought that was because I had perhaps somewhat overemphasized them in my verses."

No doubt she did ask because of his verses, but also because she wanted to know. At every stage of cognition, specific, general, and abstract, she wanted to know about birds. She even felt her fancy drawn toward a purely mythological bird, the phoenix, of whom (in "Epitaph for the Race of Man," late sonnets), she wrote:

> *These sunken cities, tier on tier, bespeak*
> *How ever from the ashes with proud beak*
> *And shining feathers did the phoenix rise,*
> *And sail, and send the vulture from the skies . . .*
> *That in the end returned.*

Her death, as I have said, came between the birds and the poets: the former she fed, the latter fed her, and she was on the stairs between them when her heart failed. In the physical rhythm of creation, by which the dust of a Caesar may nourish the roots of a bean flower, Edna subsisted literally—received sustenance and gave it—between the poets and the birds, birds and poets. This is not to say that her human affections were not strong, or that she was at all lacking in that passion which is the subject of a great part of her work, but rather in a quintessential sense that what set her apart from other women (or even from other poets) was a directness of translation between the two.

All lyric poets, it may be supposed, have some degree of suspicion that what they do relates them to that one creature we know which has as the law of its being to sing and to fly. And yet they vary astonishingly in the expression of this feeling: in Walt Whitman it appears hardly at all, and you can read great quantities of his work in which no bird sings even by indirection, even by the most devious reference. In a general way it is the Elizabethans and the Romantics who have the strongest awareness of that kinship and express it most often, either directly or by implication. In some—as in Shelley's "To a Skylark" —it goes to the extreme and asserts that the bird cannot be a bird, but must, in fact, be a poet *in excelsis*:

> *Bird thou never wert—*
> *That from heaven or near it*
> *Pourest thy full heart*
> *In profuse strains of unpremeditated art.*

When the bird is absent he still haunts the Elizabethans and the Romantics. Thus it is in Keats' "La Belle Dame sans Merci"—

> *The sedge is wither'd from the lake,*
> *And no birds sing.*

Thus it is in one of the most beloved of Shakespeare's sonnets:

> *That time of year thou may'st in me behold*
> *When yellow leaves, or none, or few, do hang*

The Indigo Bunting

Upon those boughs which shake against the cold—
Bare ruin'd choirs where late the sweet birds sang.

The Elizabethans even imitated bird song in their verse. Witness Shakespeare's cuckoo, his "tu-whit, tu-who!" and "hey ding-a-ding, ding," and "cock-a-diddle-dow." Or Thomas Nashe: "Cuckoo, jug-jug, pu-we, to-witta-woo!" Other examples might come to mind from Thomas Dekker, from Heywood, and from Fletcher, but not from John Donne: decorum had already invaded.

With the Romantics there are assigned human or suprahuman values to the birds: it is Shelley, Keats, and their progeny, among whom Tennyson must surely be one, who transfer their own sadness or joy into the forest song. Shelley's skylark was, of course, his own poetic genius: Keats' nightingale, with its metempsychosis, arouses his own nostalgia to join the bird in another world on "the viewless wings of Poesy." The simplicity and directness of the Elizabethans has here grown introspective and has taken on a melancholy which at times approaches despair—despair at the inability to merge one life into many or at least into a containing reality of high-and-low, past-and-present. (This seems to me the essential romantic despair: it is not much different in France, Italy, Germany, or anywhere, and it speaks as clearly through Leopardi as through De Musset.)

Edna Millay accepted all the poets as she accepted all the birds: none was without interest to her. And yet it seems to me that her directness of response to her natural environment was much more Elizabethan than Romantic. At her best she was

never self-conscious about the earth-forces she felt so strongly—
she did not trouble to "complicate the modeling," as the clever
people say, or to give the slightest overtone or undertone to a
simple statement of natural event:

> *The cuckoo spoke from out the wood,*
> *The lark from out the sky.*

These two lines, apparently plain facts within the competence
of any child to state, have a curious magic. Only today, in listening to Beethoven's second Razumovsky quartet, at the beginning
of the wonderful slow movement (*adagio molto*) I was put ir-
resistibly in mind of these apparently simple lines. The 'cello
sings from out the wood—a cuckoo song, plainly—and the
violin mounts high above in a larklike movement of indescribable
beauty. Beethoven, too, was expressing directly, without the
slightest self-consciousness, what he felt to be the plain statement
of an experience. His friend Holtz tells us that this movement
was written after an all-night meditation over the Baden valley
near Vienna. Perhaps: but whatever it was, Edna Millay also
seized it in two childlike statements. It is as different from the
hermetic lines of some modern poets (such as the T. S. Eliot of
the 1920's), which require more explanatory notes than there is
actual body of verse, as the Wagnerian tapestry is from Mozart.
She was therefore, and I doubt if anybody could deny it, closer
to the earlier poets than she was to those rather elaborate composers (Shelley, Keats, and afterward Hopkins) whom she most
constantly admired throughout her life. It is difficult for me to
detect in her lyrics and sonnets, with the possible exception of

the "Ode to Silence," any direct influence from Shelley or Keats.
No doubt it is there: it must be there because those poets dwelt
in her consciousness more persistently than any other except the
one whom all writers of English absorb with the language itself.
But whatever they did to her does not appear on the surface.
There is no imitation that can be discerned.

I think there was some direct imitation, at the very beginning,
but of Shakespeare, not of any other. She has herself reprinted,
in the foreword to her *Collected Sonnets,* one which she wrote
at the age of fifteen. She gives it as "an object of possible curiosity," but it is in fact a very passable sonnet, metrically skilful and
full of feeling, even though it is the rather surprising feeling of
a young girl burning love letters "yellow with age." In this early
example we feel sure that Shakespeare's sonnets have been her
fare for a good while, that she has taken them into her idiosyncratic metronome at the very heart's core: that they are part of
her. I never heard her say any sonnets of Shakespeare aloud, and
regret that very much: she must have had a deeper emotional
bond with them than with other poetry.

Her sonnets are mostly Shakespearean, some Petrarchan. The
form is regular iambic pentameter with octaves and sestets vary-
ing in the Shakespearean manner as to rhyme scheme; there were
three written in tetrameter (in *Huntsman, What Quarry?*) but
when she came to make up the volumes of *Collected Lyrics* and
Collected Sonnets she put these into the former, not the latter.
The feeling is also Elizabethan enough, in its constant reference
to nature as frame of reference and court of appeal for human
love, and there are times, especially in the earlier ones, when

Shakespeare is brought vividly to mind. The very first sonnet in *Renascence* (published when she was twenty-five, but undoubtedly written much earlier) begins:

> *Thou art not lovelier than lilacs,—no,*
> *Nor honeysuckle; thou art not more fair*
> *Than small white single poppies,—I can bear*
> *Thy beauty.*

No reader could fail to be reminded of Shakespeare's

> *My mistress' eyes are nothing like the sun,*
> *Coral is far more red than her lips' red. . . .*

The calling up of this overwhelming forebear never occurs again quite so plainly, even though there are many sonnets in which Shakespeare's pulse seems to echo from afar. (It would be difficult to write anything in the "English" sonnet form which did not to some extent beat in that way.) There is a lovely one in *The Harp-Weaver* which begins:

> *I know I am but summer to your heart,*
> *And not the full four seasons of the year.*

Others could be adduced. But there are a large number in which, although the Shakespearean form is intact, the content is of a sort that could never have been written in Shakespeare's day or, as it seems to me, by anybody but Edna. Such a one is this, which I quote entire:

> *Still will I harvest beauty where it grows:*
> *In coloured fungus and the spotted fog*
> *Surprised on foods forgotten; in ditch and bog*

The Indigo Bunting

Filmed brilliant with irregular rainbows
Of rust and oil, where half a city throws
Its empty tins; and in some spongy log
Whence headlong leaps the oozy emerald frog. ....
And a black pupil in the green scum shows.
Her the inhabiter of divers places
Surmising at all doors, I push them all.
Oh, you that fearful of a creaking hinge
Turn back forevermore with craven faces,
I tell you Beauty bears an ultra fringe
Unguessed of you upon her gossamer shawl!

With few exceptions, then, her Shakespearean form does not involve imitation and does not evoke a too specific memory of the poet who animates all English writing. The filiation is still beyond denial. It arises not only from form and from the Elizabethan cast of Edna's own imagination, but from some inevitable similarity of emotion. Both her sonnets and his were addressed to male lovers for the most part, with very considerable emphasis upon male beauty. This alone is enough to make a similarity, since practically all other love sonnets known to us are addressed either to abstractions or to women. In the case of Petrarch, of course, we have both: the sonnets *In Vita di Madonna Laura* are addressed to a woman, even though he scarcely knew her, and the ones *In Morte di Madonna Laura* are elegiac or abstract.

There is little that is abstract about Edna Millay's sonnets: they are as directly addressed as Shakespeare's and seem to have the same vital connection with experience. Shakespeare's "lovely boy," to whom some three-quarters of his sonnets are addressed,

82

was obviously one and one only, as his "dark lady" (who got the other quarter and with it, apparently, the "lovely boy") was one and one only. Edna's "unremembered lads" are frankly plural, and much of her verse concerns the ease with which she forgets them. There is, however, in most of her sonnets, a dwelling upon male beauty and male passion which is not to be found in English outside of Shakespeare. (In Italian it occurs, notably in the sonnets of Michelangelo; those he addressed to boys are passionate and those to Vittoria Colonna are platonic in tone.)

Furthermore, Edna also seems to have written love sonnets to women. It would be difficult to interpret otherwise the one beginning:

> *Love is not blind. I see with single eye*
> *Your ugliness and other women's grace.*

It is, by and large, this preoccupation with physical beauty which makes the content of Edna Millay's sonnets seem as Shakespearean as their form; and it may be (why not?) that this was the reason why nature pulled or drove her into her lifelong devotion to that form. Its dimensions permit of the kind of intensity, brief and poignant, which was native to her. Of the very great sonnet writers, Petrarch, Ronsard, Shakespeare, Milton, and Wordsworth (to whom Germans would probably add August von Platen), there can hardly be one who was more fully at ease, at home, natural and unbound, in this small and uncompromising form, which even her beloved Shelley found too tight to hold his wings. In her *Collected Sonnets* there are one hundred and sixty-one examples, and in almost none of them is the reader conscious of any fetters upon the natural play of her gift.

Amongst them are to be found some lighter in tone than is usual with sonnets (even hers): for the form has appealed, through many centuries, to the passions of love and grief rather than to any cooler sense. The one beginning "The light comes back with Columbine" (from *The Harp-Weaver*) is such a one; so is the one which begins "I shall forget you presently, my dear" (from *A Few Figs from Thistles*) with its ending:

> *Whether or not we find what we are seeking*
> *Is idle, biologically speaking.*

This ease within the "narrow room" of a most rigid form was acquired, of course, through familiarity with models and through endless practice, after the discovery (perhaps unconscious or through Shakespeare half-conscious) that this was congenial to her natural gift. I have an idea that Edna wrote more sonnets which she never published—and no doubt destroyed—than she ever published. I also know, from my one visit to the poetry room, that she was amply acquainted with the work of all who wrote sonnets from Guittone d'Arezzo onward. My discovery in that respect I have already dwelt upon: she lived, at least in part, amongst the poets of all languages. The French sonneteers of the Renaissance were well known to her, as well as the original Italians; this was perhaps not so astonishing as it seemed to me (I had met so few people in my own country who knew anything about Italian poetry that I was unduly startled, had not sufficiently taken in how deeply poetry *was* her life). But I think I was entitled to surprise when I found that she also knew the sonnets of Filicaia, which, at the end of the seventeenth century, did somewhat revive the glories of the form in Italy but have been forgotten elsewhere. I have a notion that she possessed, within her cavernous memory, an enormous treasure of sonnets which she could cull over in her mind with the inner voices that never failed her. The resource was invaluable for all poetry (in illness, for instance) but she could not have moved so indigenously in sonnet form, like a fish in a brook, if she had not largely taken into her system the whole singing reliquary of the past.

And she was in her poetry, of course, specifically a woman. There are some of her sonnets, as well as a good many of her lyrics, which might be read as being the work of a man, but these do not govern. For the most part she wrote as a woman, and after some acquaintance with her work the reader generalizes this (the greater part) over all the rest, so that it all seems woman just as it all seems poet. The gist, she says, is this:

> *I, being born a woman and distressed*
> *By all the needs and notions of my kind,*
> *Am urged by your propinquity to find*
> *Your person fair, and feel a certain zest*
> *To bear your body's weight upon my breast.*

This being so, it is strange that I not only never heard her speak of a woman poet, but have not heard that she ever did so, the exception being her friend Elinor Wylie: but there it was the friend, not the poet, who came to mind. She did not talk of Emily Dickinson or Elizabeth Barrett Browning, although their verses were familiar to her, as I know from her library; Christina Rossetti was another who lived on her shelves but not, so far as hours of talk might show, in her mind. The truth is that all these women poets were spinsterish in a high degree, which Edna never was. The one woman poet who did kindle her imagination was Sappho, in whose voice she speaks in "Evening on Lesbos" (from *The Buck in the Snow*) and "Sappho Crossed the Dark River into Hades" (*Wine from These Grapes*). For a good many years there was a bust of Sappho in the living room at Steepletop; it was a gift from Italy. I believe her Greek was good enough to derive pleasure and profit from reading Greek poetry, and of course the fragments of Sappho have been repeatedly translated into modern languages; but even so I believe that it was the idea of Sappho, rather than the actually surviving verse, which called to her across time. Explicit passion on the part of a woman writer of poetry has been so completely unknown in English that it is no wonder this poet, indubitably born of this and no other language, had in her fire and tears to turn back to Greece.

And inconstancy, which is so much a part of all poetry in classical ages, was again an element native to Edna but only sporadic (and then only among men) in English verse. Her work is filled with assurances that she will forget the "not impossible him" to whom she wrote so much, or that she has in fact already forgotten. The return to the Greeks, in feeling, is a return to two springs: Sappho and the Greek anthology. She loves and forgets and loves again, sometimes even scorning the physical passion which is the stuff of her song. Thus the cold conclusion of the sonnet "I, being born a woman":

The Birds

Think not for this . . .
I shall remember you with love, or season
My scorn with pity,—let me make it plain:
I find this frenzy insufficient reason
For conversation when we meet again.

One sonnet from *The Harp-Weaver* expresses to the full the recurring inconstancy for which English poetry gave her little warrant and which, therefore, helped to turn her back to the Greeks. It is:

What lips my lips have kissed, and where, and why,
I have forgotten, and what arms have lain
Under my head till morning; but the rain
Is full of ghosts tonight, that tap and sigh
Upon the glass and listen for reply,
And in my heart there stirs a quiet pain
For unremembered lads that not again
Will turn to me at midnight with a cry.
Thus in the winter stands the lonely tree,
Nor knows what birds have vanished one by one,
Yet knows its boughs more silent than before:
I cannot say what loves have come and gone,
I only know that summer sang in me
A little while, that in me sings no more.

Here the sestet presents us with the poet as a lonely tree which remembers the music and the summer, but not the single birds. It is this theme to which Edna Millay, belated Greek as she sometimes seems to be, returns more times than to any other in her work, and it is no doubt this which gave her the *succès de scandale* which seems to have been hers in the 1920's. (I remember only echoes of it, since I was living in Europe while it went on, but others remember it vividly.) She sang as her nature bade her, but since such themes had never been made the subject of English poetry by a woman before, and seldom in modern times by a man, the shocked delight of the drawing rooms can easily be imagined.

And Greek, too, is the extreme simplicity of her language, which in all probability would make her impossible to translate into any foreign tongue with good effect. When we survey the disasters which have fallen upon all (even Swinburne) who have made any attempt to render Sappho's stanzas into English verse, we may guess at the flat inconsequence which would result if Edna's songs were put into French or German. How could this be anything but English?

> *It's little I care what path I take,*
> *And where it leads it's little I care;*
> *But out of this house, lest my heart break,*
> *I must go, and off somewhere.*

Or again:

> *If I could have*
> *   Two things in one:*
> *The peace of the grave,*
> *   And the light of the sun.*

Or once more:

The Birds

Boys and girls that lie
Whispering in the hedges,
Do not let me die,
Mix me with your pledges;
Boys and girls that slowly walk
In the woods, and weep, and quarrel,
Staring past the pink wild laurel,
Mix me with your talk.

There at the top of the stairs at Steepletop she had the reassurance she needed. Whatever her complexities of joy and woe, she found that her kindred in the poetry room were not strangers to them. In many times and places, in dialects spoken no more, in languages strange to today's ear or even yesterday's, poets had felt and expressed that which was later to be expressed again in the clear English of Shakespeare, Wordsworth, Shelley, and Keats, and which no doubt Edna felt would be expressed anew whenever the urge came upon a bursting throat. Her kindred in the trees outside—and on the ground too, for she records quite proudly in the *Bird Guide* that no less than fourteen different species of birds at Steepletop one summer nested *on the ground* —sang by a simpler law of being, but those in the poetry room obeyed a compulsion equally mysterious and imperative. This, the compulsion, to which obedience at times might seem a form of slavery, was so supreme a law that when it ceased, as it had done when I saw Edna at Ragged Island, her impersonal misery engulfed the world. Whatever their dimensions they were like-natured there in the poetry room, as were the purple and yellow and scarlet and blue creatures that paused on the window sill on their way to the cool green north or the blazing south. From the one as from the other she drew life and with them reached up toward the sky.

Of all the remarks Heinrich Heine made during his long struggle to become a Parisian wit, the most foolish, it seems to me, is what he said of Berlioz after hearing that composer's *Requiem*. Berlioz, he said, was "a lark as big as an eagle." That would be, in other words, a monster. An eagle is as big as an eagle and a lark is as big as a lark, nor would wisdom have it otherwise. In the delicate adjustments of a world which we may perceive to be only a concourse of atoms, tremulous with potential departure, each form and color and sound has for its moment (the moment of our lives) an inevitability in time-space whenever it is true and can be powerfully, intuitively felt to be true. It is the truth that communicates and is self-evident. Who, then, would wish for an eagle in the presence of a lark? There in the wet hedgerow dwell the possible flight, the possible song, which when they occur pierce the heart like an arrow. The eagle—let it be Dante; let it be Homer—may glower majestically on his craggy height and command us as he will, for we must obey, whether we would or not: such is his power. But Shakespeare knew that the arrowy music, swifter and briefer,

> *Like to the lark at break of day arising*
> *From sullen earth sings hymns at heaven's gate.*

4

The Bird

IN THE parabasis of his comedy, Aristophanes gives free rein
to all the luxuriant fancies of an Athenian wit as it was per-
mitted to flourish in that golden time. *The Birds* may not be the
finest of comedies, but it is one in which a variety of once-sacred
things come into their own as comic material; and it is certain
that it would not have seemed audacious in the eyes of the
Athenian populace if there had not existed a sneaking notion
that the things were still sacred, really, even though it was the
fashion of the city to make fun of them. City dwellers, after all,
especially Athenians, up-to-date in all matters and expert in
sacrilege, practiced at adultery and pederasty alike, irreverent
toward rulers and ruled, strategus and taxiarch, philosopher and
tragedian, could not be expected to accept the rustic superstitions
of their forefathers who dwelt in the forest and to whom the
bird or the birds, all birds, carried a special message from the
divine powers and conveyed augury and omen to such men as
were capable of understanding. These beliefs were well known

to the Athenians and were never, even in the time of Aristophanes, disavowed; in fact, the very word *ornis*, which meant bird, also meant omen. But the parabasis of the comedy, in which the chorus and two semichoruses recite the cosmogony of the birds, their origin as the childen of Eros before gods and men, their supernal powers, missions, and benefactions, and the advantages that might accrue to any man who saw fit to join them, is the hyperbolical statement in the terms of Aristophanes, full of zest and physicality, of something all Greeks really did, in their hearts, believe. They might leave the theater in delighted laughter, saying to each other, "How shocked my grandfather would have been!" but in truth they did not differ much from that grandfather in the groundwork of reference to their natural environment.

And the birds, of course, were the divine messengers. In every age of Greece they had brought signs of destiny, had spoken warning, prophecy, and promise. Just as the serpent symbolized the soul in its earth-bound aspect, and was so treated in the religious mysteries and representations, so the bird represented the spiritual elevation of the human soul, its communication with the divine to which it belonged. In fact, when Aristophanes makes his comic Pithetaerus say: "Formerly men always swore by the birds and never by the gods," he was putting into hyperbole something that fundamentally could not seem particularly unreasonable to any Greek. The war between the birds and the gods, although wildly funny to the Athenian audience, bore that precise relation to the conceived reality which makes comedy possible—if it had not been comprehensibly akin to notions seriously entertained in the view of life, its exaggeration and caricature could not have been funny at all.

And when we go back beyond that skeptical and metropolitan age we find the literal acceptance of the bird as divine messenger in so many times and places that it becomes what for practical purposes is called "universal." It is not really universal, of course, since we know too little of this or adjacent universes to make the term applicable; but it is at least general in mankind. It occurs in the evidences offered by archaeology, mythology, and anthropology at widely separated places in centuries far from each other: in ancient Egypt and India, in the valley of the Euphrates and Tigris, among the Norsemen and the Druids, the aboriginal inhabitants of the New World and the primitive cultures still in existence today. There cannot be any doubt that human beings have always shown an instinctual awe of two things, flight and song, which are the special secret of the birds: flight because its swiftness, its independence of earth-obstacles, abashes man's impotence with envy and wonder, and song not because of sensuous beauty alone, but because it appears to contain a language which men do not understand.

So the whole baggage of the past is filled with mementoes of this awe of man for bird. It comes into almost innumerable stories of the most ancient date. The legendary king Vikramaditya, in ancient India, owed much of his prowess to the fact that he could understand the language of the birds, who were always revealing to him the nature of future dangers. One of the stories of Apollodorus—told also by others—has to do with the wise man who had learned the language of the birds through the kindness of some serpents whose lives he had saved. This theme is very widespread: the serpent, the earth-bound soul, was nevertheless a soul and could therefore understand the language of the ethereal soul, the bird. Thus it is that the learning of bird language by drinking a serpent's blood (or eating a serpent's flesh) is common to such a variety of folk tales. It is said on the authority of Saxo Grammaticus that the philosopher Democritus actually advised this method of learning the birds' secrets. Pliny, too, tells such tales (of Arabs and of Indians). The one most familiar to modern westerners is that from the Eddas which Richard Wagner used in his *Siegfried*: the hero Sigurd (renamed Siegfried) kills the dragon Fafnir, and upon tasting his heart's blood knows at once how to understand the birds. (Operagoers would remember that Wagner's Siegfried addresses the dragon as "Wurm," or serpent.)

There is almost no limit to the number of stories which betray the persuasion of man, in all his simpler states of being, that the bird has been sent to tell him something. The bird is also an omen, suggesting good or ill fortune, or sent as a warning; the bird is a divine attribute, belongs to some particular god; the bird is itself divine; the bird betokens luck for some particular crop or for all crops.

In North America one of the most curious of tribal ceremonies grew up over the journeys of migratory waterfowl. Certain North American Indian tribes believed that The Old Woman Who Never Dies (an earth-mother goddess, of course, a sort of prototype of the majestic Demeter) controlled the crops, lived in the south, and sent the migratory waterfowl as her representatives seasonally. The wild goose patronized the maize, the wild swan the gourds, the wild duck was propitious for the beans. The old women of the tribe, representing the Old Woman Who Never Dies, officiated at magic ceremonies in a spring festival held whenever these migrants began to appear.

And examples could be multiplied. The point is not that primitive man believed such things, or that contemporary primitives still believe them (as among the Dyaks of Borneo), but that a weight of evidence has accumulated in modern psychology and goes on accumulating to the effect that beliefs held so widely and deeply, over what must have been an immense stretch of human time, have left a residue in the consciousness of civilized mankind, in its treasures of symbol even in the unconscious, and in its instinctive behavior. We do not have to follow too closely the working of psychological method to see that this is extremely probable, or to perceive that analysis based upon it is likely to yield coherent results. Such has, in fact, been the case with those numerous followers of Dr. Carl Jung, for instance, who have applied to myth, folklore, and transmitted legend a theory which gives depth and contemporary vitality to their course in all ages and among all peoples.

The thing is self-evident among children. We can see it for ourselves whenever we have an opportunity to watch children with birds. The attempt of the child to talk to the bird and to understand its language (or to interpret it) is universal. But even grown men and women show in innumerable ways the vestiges of a belief which is obviously natural to the human race. I have heard farmers in both southern and northern states of the United States declare with all confidence that this or that bird "says" it is going to rain, to get colder or hotter, or that a storm is coming. And I have also observed that the event sometimes justifies the prediction, sometimes not; but whether it does or not, the farmer's faith is not shaken; he will repeat the same things the next time.

Bird as omen is a grown-up belief, particularly among farmers, sailors, and hunters nowadays; bird as soul-with-a-secret, as messenger, seems to be natural to children; but bird-as-creature-set-apart is common to almost all imaginative human beings. A wealth of ordinary experience confirms this. Hardly anybody speaks of birds in the same way as of other animals; bird watching and bird listening are pursuits which with a good many men and women become a primary interest in life; the use of birds as symbols is current and accepted, taken for granted, by the generality of mankind. When at the outset of the Holy Year of 1950 the Sovereign Pontiff in Rome released a cloud of white doves over the Piazza di San Pietro he was touching off a symbolism which is extremely old, sanctioned by many religions, and rooted in more direct beliefs in primitive man. The Holy Ghost itself is symbolized in Roman Catholic art and iconography by a dove. It has been pointed out by Gilbert Murray in *The Early Stages of Greek Religion* that whenever a god or goddess has an animal as attribute (in fairly late stages) it is safe to assume that the animal was the original object of worship and the anthropomorphic divinity was added afterward. Thus it was with Athena and her owl—and the owl has remained, in literature and in the imaginations of most civilized men, in symbolic association with wisdom.

It appears to me that those among us—excluding scientists—

who devote very special attention and time to birds are sensitive and imaginative human beings with a little more communicative gift, so far as nonhumans are concerned, than the rest of us. It is a matter of general knowledge that birds do come to such persons more than they do to others. How or why is another question: it cannot be resolved simply by referring it to food, although food is an element. We have in a village in Vermont, near the farm where I live, one such bird lover. He is an elderly man who lives alone and has a small thicket of trees behind his house. He feeds the birds, it is true, but nothing could explain the thronging of the tribe to his small thicket in the times of migration.

Such men and women have an inclination toward solitude, and in their solitude the songs, colors, habits, migration and return of the birds assume enormous significance. I have never penetrated the secrets of such minds, but I am convinced that to them there *is* a communication with the birds, that it goes two ways, and that it would never be possible to express it sanely or intelligibly in language. In other words, to be quite frank, I regard it as a form of mystical experience. It shares with other mystical experiences (such as art, love, and the perception of the divine) the quality of being what is called "ineffable," i.e., beyond explanation in words.

If it is a mystical experience, as my observation makes me believe, then the relation of man and bird, when it is established, verifies all the old beliefs of all the peoples everywhere, and the bird becomes in fact (for just those persons and no others) a divine messenger. The bird becomes for certain persons what he once was for all persons. This is not to suggest that such persons are in any way "insane" or even abnormal (that bogey of the imaginative and the solitary). They have merely developed an extra sense which opens to them an experience the rest of us cannot share and can never fully understand because it cannot be explained.

With Edna St. Vincent Millay all that I have here indicated was true but she was reluctant to face it as statement of fact. I never saw anybody who behaved more like an instinctive and unreflecting pantheist, and the fact is spread across her entire written work, from the first. In *Renascence,* for example, what is this girl who worships God in the earth and in the sky as she flings herself upon the hillside? Is she not a form or aspect of Goethe's *Ganymed* or of any other impulse of pantheism in the universe? What is her desire, and how does she treat the one and the many? This is how it ends:

> *The world stands out on either side*
> *No wider than the heart is wide;*
> *Above the world is stretched the sky,—*
> *No higher than the soul is high.*
> *The heart can push the sea and land*
> *Farther away on either hand;*
> *The soul can split the sky in two,*
> *And let the face of God shine through.*
> *But East and West will pinch the heart*
> *That can not keep them pushed apart;*
> *And he whose soul is flat—the sky*
> *Will cave in on him by and by.*

If the heart and soul are expressed by earth and sky, and are in fact conterminous with them, how does this differ from classical pantheism, an enormous part (much the largest) of Hindu philosophy, the "transcendentalism" of New England in the nineteenth century, and in fact all those other apperceptions and expressions of unity which have persisted throughout man's record here? I see no difference, and when Edna shied at the direct statements she was, I think, only doing so in fear of being led too far—in being led to state that which she preferred to leave only implied. I remember how she laughed once when I accused her of being a Hindu for using the phrase "Destroyer and Preserver." I told her that this particular binomialism was specifically Hindu; perhaps I mentioned Shiva; in any case I remember her answer.

"I don't know a thing about Shiva," she said. "When I use the phrase it's straight out of Shelley, and that's its only origin."

But her readers will think without trouble of innumerable instances in her work which strongly indicate the possession of a sense of identity with the creatures which, of all animate nature, most obsessed her imagination. I have given some examples: the nightingale in Sonnet XX of *Fatal Interview* becomes indistinguishable from the poet-lover in the sestet. Song and flight are not things done to the poet: they are the poet. Less direct is the "projection," as the psychologists call it, of the poet ino the bird, so that the bird becomes an aspect of the poet's aspiration: this is seen in a pure state in "Wild Swans" (*Second April*).

> *I looked in my heart while the wild swans went over.*
> *And what did I see I had not seen before?*
> *Only a question less or a question more;*
> *Nothing to match the flight of wild birds flying.*

The Indigo Bunting

Tiresome heart, forever living and dying,
House without air, I leave you and lock your door.
Wild swans, come over the town, come over
The town again, trailing your legs and crying!

In "Pueblo Pot," again—from *The Buck in the Snow*—there are two "projections," the broken pot of many-colored shards and the "two Navajos enchanted, the red-shafted flicker and his bride." In the end of this poem, when the youth, beauty, and strength of the birds had refused to "solace the broken pot," the poet is left "to the comfort of grief" although the colors of the shards "had faded in the fierce light of the birds." The two projections vanish; the poet is left alone.

And as for the birds, they were gone. As suddenly as
they had come, they went.

This poem is a little long for quotation in full, but there is scarcely another example to be found which makes the process clearer; mysterious though the origin of the process may be, its working is apparent here.

We quote it all, therefore:

There as I bent above the broken pot from the mesa pueblo,
Mournfully many times its patterned shards piecing together and
    laying aside,
Appeared upon the house-top, two Navajos enchanted, the red-
    shafted flicker and his bride,
And stepped with lovely stride
To the pergola, flashing the wonder of their underwings;

The Bird

There stood, mysterious and harsh and sleek,
Wrenching the indigo berry from the shedding woodbine with strong
     ebony beak.

His head without a crest
Wore the red full moon for crown;
The black new moon was crescent on the breast of each;
From the bodies of both a visible heat beat down,
And from the motion of their necks a shadow would fly and fall,
Skimming the court and in the yellow adobe wall
Cleaving a blue breach.

Powerful was the beauty of these birds.
It boomed like a struck bell in the silence deep and hot.
I stopped above the shattered clay; passionately I cried to the beauty
     of these birds,
"Solace the broken pot!"

The beauty of these birds
Opened its lips to speak;
Colours were its words,
The scarlet shaft on the grey cheek,
The purple berry in the ebony beak.
It said: "I cannot console
The broken thing; I can only make it whole."

Wisdom, heretic flower, I was ever afraid
Of your large, cool petals without scent!
Shocked, betrayed,
I turned to the comfort of grief, I bent
Above the lovely shards.
But their colours had faded in the fierce light of the birds.

And as for the birds, they were gone. As suddenly as they had come, they went.

Here we see the projections actually occurring: the birds and the shards are originally things observed, described, and it is only in the third stanza that the poem itself (poet and reader with it) become both. This is, of course, on the conscious level; beneath that there can be little doubt that the whole concept is from the recesses of the poet's being and is therefore a projection from beginning to end. It is so of many poems, all those, in fact, which are not simply descriptive, but the working out of the spiritual or psychological phenomenon is not so dramatically presented elsewhere.

Simple descriptive verse abounds in English more than in any other language, I believe: a great part of the work of a great poet, Wordsworth, is in this kind. I do not suggest that whenever Edna Millay writes of her birds she becomes or expresses them by some hocus-pocus of identification: not at all. She achieves external description as well and as often as the next one, and has, in fact, a very special knack in the matter. Anybody who has seen her bird book knows that she did observe keenly and well. That guide contains some mysterious code-signals which only she could know, crosses and circles and the like, but it also has, as I have shown, some very matter-of-fact notations. And her poems are full of things vividly seen and heard from the outside. One lovely bit of sound-weaving, which she calls simply "Counting-out Rhyme," is pure description:

The Bird

Silver bark of beech, and sallow
Bark of yellow birch and yellow
Twig of willow.

Stripe of green in moosewood maple,
Colour seen in leaf of apple,
Bark of popple.

Wood of popple pale as moonbeam,
Wood of oak for yoke and barn-beam,
Wood of hornbeam.

Silver bark of beech, and hollow
Stem of elder, tall and yellow
Twig of willow.

And description, observation, the delicate perception of visible beauty meant as much to her as to all or most poets: it seemed at times to be more essential to her being, or at any rate more permanent, than any emotion. Thus she says ("The Wood Road," from *The Harp-Weaver and Other Poems*):

If I were to walk this way
Hand in hand with Grief,
I should mark that maple-spray
Coming into leaf.
I should note how the old burrs
Rot upon the ground.
Yes, though Grief should know me hers
While the world goes round,
It could not in truth be said
This was lost on me:

The Indigo Bunting

A rock-maple showing red
Burrs beneath a tree.

There are to be discerned several degrees of absorption in
nature on the part of those whose writing is part conscious skill
and partly unconscious projection: Edna Millay's verse shows
the whole range of it, from almost unalloyed observation to complete identity. She did not like to say that all life was one, and
she acknowledged with difficulty any special sensitivity of her
own to other forms of life, but in her daily acts as in her writing
she betrayed the awareness. It appears to me that in so doing she
bore witness to an ancient kinship, not only with poets long dead,
but also with island peasants and fishermen, rustic queens and
oracles, lone men in the darkling wood, girls dancing in moon-
light—all those creatures of anonymous time before history
began to be written, before the self-consciousness of man had
concentrated the idea of divinity into anthropomorphic idols. If
the learned can seek out for us, as they have done, evidences of
men's belief in a spirit informing all life, with the bird as its
messenger or spokesman, we can cap their learning with examples from the existence we share even in this late day: we find
it abundantly around us, and those who feel it are not all poets.
(Pagans they may be, in the antique sense, but not all are poets.)
One, however, was. Rising at dawn—or before going to bed at
dawn—with her red hair flying loose and her green eyes gleam-
ing, this gentle pagan stalked her beloved messengers, talking to
them, listening to them, feeding them, sitting on the ground in
motionless absorption as she watched them while the first light

brought into being the brave flash of their many colors, and it is not for me to say that she did not have some comprehension of what they told her, or that they in their turn did not somehow understand her. Whether it was by way of the serpent's blood is another question, but I saw that the communication existed. If our language is too poor to contain it, that is our misfortune. Flight to these companions and delight in their song was not so much an escape from humanity as an extension of it—a recognition of the larger life from which ours, too, comes, and into which it is taken in due course again, to be manifested in ways we can never begin to guess, but perhaps even in flight, perhaps in song.

5

Habitat

STEEPLETOP, where Edna St. Vincent Millay lived for twenty-five years, is a farmhouse made over without undue luxury into a comfortable modern dwelling. To see it first deep in verdure, as I did, especially at a time of so much rain, is to get an unreal impression of isolation. It is actually only a mile off a main highway (Route 22) and there are other houses not far away. Mr. John Pinnie, the farmer and her devoted friend, lives down the slope. Edna had a desire for solitude which grew with the years and eventually engulfed even the telephone, so that it used to be necessary to send messages to her through the general store at the village of Austerlitz.

But to see it bare in winter, with the branches naked against white snow, produces a clearer impression of its grace and relation to its surroundings. It belongs in its own landscape, winter or summer, and the tutelary genius of the place had made no effort to change that relation. She was, when she went to Steepletop, in her early thirties; she had already published, with an initial success seldom granted to any poet, several volumes of her best work. She had apparently from childhood the mythogenic, mythopoeic, legendary quality which clung to her through life, and wherever she went she trailed the spread plumage of other people's stories. (I believe there was a period in the 1920's when stories were invented and attached to her name, just as witticisms in addition to her own were attributed to Miss Dorothy Parker.) There are always a few persons in the national life of the United States who seem to disseminate legend by the mere act of being alive, although most of them do have some more solid reason for existence. Mark Twain was one such before the present time; the sayings attributed to him in our parents' days were far more numerous than any one man could have invented. Much legend has concentrated on a few film stars, and there was an era when certain opera singers were truly legendary (as distinct from being merely famous). Among politicians a few had the myth-making knack, too, and lived in an aura of their own making, conscious or unconscious. There are two remarks it might be useful to make about American mythology of this kind, since Edna Millay was part of it: first, that the phenomenon flourishes mainly by word of mouth and does not usually reach print; second, that the American people, who create the mythology, are not themselves aware of how they do it or why. It is easy to assign reasons afterward, but while it is going on there is a kind of mystery in this spontaneous generation of tales the people love to tell.

Willa Cather, in one of her wise and sensitive stories about opera singers, advances the hypothesis that the Americans' love for legend about living characters (and the American talent for creating such legends) is based upon the desire to make a substitute "royal family" for the nation. It may be so. At all events there has never been a time in the present century when there were not a dozen or more real, living people who had somehow or other become the center of innumerable stories circulated from one end of the country to the other. It seems to have nothing to do with fame or fortune or even that slippery yardstick called "success." Many persons still in middle life can remember when Isadora Duncan, whose fortune had evaporated and whose "success" was nonexistent, lived in almost a state of suffocation from her own legend. If your own life happens to have brought you into some relation, close or far, with the objects of this storytelling solicitude, you will experience often one of the oddest of all sensations, which is to hear something quite vivid, apparently intimate, and obviously false being told aloud by total strangers about a person you know well.

Edna was one of these persons, and must have learned quite early in her life that the only means of continuing existence on terms bearable to herself was by ignoring it. For this purpose Steepletop must have been, from 1925 when she bought it until 1950 when she died there, a refuge as well as her own solid and enduring place. She did not live there all the time by any means, but she always returned there for a good part of the year, sometimes for the whole year. She loved life and the world, traveled a good deal, was fond of the sun, enjoyed very much the company of men and women who had nothing to do with literature, and probably in her youth derived a certain amount of amusement and perhaps even pleasure of a kind at the buzzing and humming of talk that surrounded her wherever she went. She could not have been unaware of the existence of a national legend about her; she was too intelligent. It happened to her very early. It had been happening ever since she first began to write verses and play the piano, as Mrs. Millay's eldest daughter ("the one with red hair and green eyes," they probably said, although her sister Norma had similar coloring), in Camden, Maine, or earlier at Rockport or Union, Maine. Perhaps, therefore, she may not have fully realized what an explosion she caused in 1920 by the publication of *A Few Figs from Thistles,* her second volume of verse. (*Renascence* was published in 1917.) The "First Fig" in the 1920 book became a sort of motto or epigraph for the whole decade that followed: it is the quatrain which begins "My candle burns at both ends." These lines were caught up and quoted, or more usually misquoted, by every jejune hedonist of the rebellious era, every girl or boy who wanted to experiment with the recently discovered benefits of alcohol, sexual experience, or simply late hours and wild talk. Scott Fitzgerald's stories bestowed a self-consciousness upon the young people of the 1920's, a self-consciousness they did not really need, but Edna in that one quatrain supplied them with a *point d'appui,* an aesthetic justification for kicking over the traces. Everybody who was alive during the 1920's must remember how rapidly all customs, manners, and ideas in American life altered during that decade of careless wealth, crumbling standards, and deliberate revolt against society. Sinclair Lewis's tremendous novels *Main Street* and *Babbitt* were a full-scale offensive by the big battalions, with all weapons used and nothing barred; but Edna's four flippant lines in 1920 were the *Marseillaise* of that particular revolution.

And the immediate, inevitable consequence was that Edna

herself became symbol, legend, almost standard-bearer, for a social upheaval which was in reality outside her interest. There has seldom been a truer lyric poet, and if I have correctly defined or circumscribed her essential life as being between the birds and the poets, it may be seen that she really had little in common with either the ambitious and volatile Fitzgerald or the essentially social phenomenon of Sinclair Lewis. All her purest work is quite timeless, and it was only the rise of Fascism that aroused her to some poems (such as those written in 1940) which are clearly of a certain hour. In the 1920's, for which she has been said to be in some respects historically responsible, she hardly seems to have noticed the social environment: her responsibility, if it exists, is the same as that of the sea gull for that oceanic wind upon which he rides.

But it did make the legend national, and wished upon her a variety of characteristics true and false which amplified her single existence in the popular imagination, made her, so to speak, larger than life. The passion of which she wrote in her poetry—and of which hardly a woman had ever dared to write—was true: it was her own. But the stories told were not content with that. They multiplied and magnified and specified and classified it all. Miss Elizabeth Atkins, in *Edna St. Vincent Millay and Her Times* (published in 1936), tells us that the poem "The Singing Woman from the Wood's Edge," which first appeared in the 1921 edition of *A Few Figs from Thistles,* was immediately supposed to be of Edna herself, and "by the time it reached Nebraska, rumor had fathered two bastard daughters on her." The process never stopped, so far as I know, and Edna's successes in the so-called "great world" of Paris, the Metropolitan Opera House, and elsewhere added new stories to the old ones until no *femme fatale* of the most lurid romancer could have carried it all.

Against this miasma, safe and sound, there were Steepletop and (later on) Ragged Island. The life there was always much as I have described it, except that there was more company at Steepletop in earlier years. That company was not of the riotous and foolish kind associated either with the 1920's or the Fitzgeralds, so far as I can tell, although Edna's appetite for festivity was obviously keen when she had the right companions. Her friends were Elinor Wylie, the Benéts, and others with whom she could talk as well as make merry. And yet even from the early years it is obvious that the essential or distinctive element of Edna's life demanded solitude and increasingly received it. Her tremendous vogue in the 1920's was something with which she had, really, very little to do; she did not create it or cultivate it, although there is no evidence that it caused her the slightest surprise; she tended, after a while, to flee from it. It seems to me that Byron, who went through the same experience, was far more affected by it: it led him into all those absurdities like shooting pistols into the Green Park on leaving England, and resenting to the end of his days everything that happened between the morning when he woke up "to find himself famous" and that departure.

Revisiting Steepletop after Edna's death was to me extraordinary in the highest degree, and for a reason which at first led me to doubt the very point of this book. It was Edna's sister Norma

(Mrs. Charles Ellis) who brought me to another view of the matter. My wife and I arrived there on the evening of February 15 of the present year, nervous and ashamed because snow and car trouble had delayed us hours beyond the time when we were expected. Norma and Charles had waited dinner for us. Everything seemed much as I remembered it, with the exception of the weather, which was as wintry as the June visit had been wet and bosky. When I came into the house, the hall, although containing other objects, was much as before. Norma led me then into the big room, which I have described in the first section, and to my pain and astonishment I saw that my memory had committed one cardinal error. The window—the big window, upon which we had been so concentrated on that week end, the window of the birds—was not at all as I remembered it, not at all as I had described it. It was simply a window precisely like every other window in that room, with four panes of glass and identical measurements.

My bewilderment was extreme. How *could* this window be just the same as all the other windows?

I still do not know how the human memory can betray a detail so badly. I walked toward it and away from it and toward the others and away from them. Nothing, nothing whatsoever, distinguished this window (the bird window) from its fellows.

To Norma I explained the shock. "I thought it was a *very* big window," I told her. "That's how I remember it and that's how I've described it. And I was wrong."

She said:

"Everything around here has diminished lately."

She had, of course, not then read what I had written about that window: but when I explained that this caused me to doubt all my memory, its accuracy to fact and relation to the truth, she said a few wise things. She told me that the window had only seemed larger than the others because it was larger to Edna, and therefore to me, and because of the coming and going of the birds, and because it was the important window in the room. She said—and repeated later, and again the next day—that I should allow the description of the window to remain as I remembered it, as a big window unlike all the others, because this contained a truth more vital than the exact measurements. She said that I could make my confession of error afterward in the book, and this is it.

But nothing, really, reveals Edna's sorcery more than this episode of the window. Because she sat by that window and looked through it, and the birds came there and looked at her, it did seem to me a very large window, exactly as I have (as faithfully as I could remember) described it. It was not so in fact, but I still think it was so in truth.

In this room, on the night of October 19, Edna had been reading the proofs of Rolfe Humphries' translation of the *Aeneid*, of which she wished to write an opinion. The galley proofs were strewn all over the floor and she had spent hours upon them. Very late, almost at dawn, she had gone to bed. She had taken with her into the hall and toward the stairs a half-bottle of Alsatian wine and a wineglass. She may or may not have fed the birds, but probably not, since it was late October. She took two steps up to the little landing where the stairs turn to go up to the library (what I have called, following her, "the poetry room") and had then sat down on the first step above the landing, carefully placing the wine on a step above. Apparently she felt faint, or in some way unable to pursue her way. She sat there on the step, leaned over, and died.

John Pinnie came in that morning as usual shortly after eight o'clock. It had been his custom for years to do so, bringing the milk, but he did not come beyond the kitchen as a rule. On this occasion he did look into the hall but saw nothing untoward and went away. Several times during the day he was in the house but did not go beyond the entrance to the hall from the kitchen. From that place it is impossible to see the turn in the stairs where Edna lay. It was three in the afternoon before he did go farther into the house and saw her. She was sitting on the first step above the landing. The bottle of wine and the wineglass were unbroken, in order, so that it is evident that she did not disturb her body when she forsook it.

The rest of the house is very much as it was, and my memory of it proves reliable in every respect except as to the bird window.

A month after her death there was a hurricane, not to be compared with the hurricane of 1938, but felt through a great part of the northeastern United States. (It fell upon the day after Thanksgiving.) This storm broke off a big tree to the left of the bird tables where Edna was accustomed to feeding her migratory friends, picked it up in the air in some weird manner and threw it across the bird tables, leaving them quite intact, and stretched the broken tree upon the other side of them. The tree, with its torn trunk and prostrate body, was still there on February 15, with the bird tables in the safe and hospitable middle.

During the course of the past winter Norma Millay has patiently worked her way through a considerable part of the great volume of material of all sorts, papers not only of Edna's but of their mother's and of the rest of the family. In doing so she came upon a poem Edna had elaborately copied out and illustrated at some very early age, perhaps at eight or so. For a long time Norma thought, as I did when it was shown to me, that this was by Edna herself; it is, as it happens, from Stevenson's *Child's Garden of Verses*; but the choice of this particular poem for her efforts is a fascinating confirmation of my theory of her affinity for the birds. It is carefully printed in pencil on ruled paper, with suitable illustrations done in colored crayon. Some of the print goes this way and some goes that way. There is one misspelling ("abor" for "arbor"—perhaps the Maine accent is responsible for that). It is boldly signed across the middle of the first page: Vincent Millay. This is the poem:

> *Birds all the sunny day*
> > *Flutter and quarrel*
> *Here in the abor-like*
> > *Tent of the laurel.*
>
> *Here in the fork*
> *The brown nest is seated*
> *Four little blue eggs*
> > *The mother keeps heated.*
>
> *While we stand watching her*
> *Staring like gabies*

The Indigo Bunting

Safe in each egg are the
Birds little babies.

VINCENT   MILLAY

Soon the frail eggs they shall
 Chip and upspringing
Make all the April woods
 Merry with singing.

Younger than we are
 O children and frailer
Soon in blue air they'll be
 Singing and sailor.

We so much older
 Taller and stronger
We shall look down on the
 Birdies no longer.

They shall go flying
With musical speeches
 High over head in the
Tops of the beeches.

In spite of our wisdom
 And sensible talking
We on our feet must go
 Plodding and walking

From a period somewhat later in their lives, at Camden, Mrs. Millay had kept, and Norma found and showed me, a schedule of the day planned for all three Millay girls by Edna, the eldest.

116

From this document, which is as solemn and detailed as the program of a ceremony in the Sistine Chapel, it is apparent that the rod of iron was (at least in theory) Edna's instrument for dealing with younger sisters. Every quarter hour of the day is rigorously apportioned for each child. "Wash dishes" or "Prepare lunch" or "Study" or "Write" or "Go into garden" are commands upheld by the authority of the clock. It was probably all a little bit Pickwickian, but it does give an indication of that curiously schoolteacherish element which was in Edna's complex and exquisite character and never altogether left her.

One sees in such bits of paper not only the memorabilia of a childhood, but also the nest-feathering of the mother. Mrs. Millay does not seem to have thrown anything away. Whatever her little brood did was interesting to her, deserved to be hoarded, and was. The Millay family came of Irish Protestant stock— Huguenot to begin with, but in Ireland since the seventeenth century—and were in Edna's childhood cultivated but poor people. Mr. Millay was superintendent of schools at Union, Maine, where the family lived shortly after Edna's birth. (She was, as has been said, born in Rockland, on Washington's Birthday in 1892.) From all I can make out, Mr. Millay had no talent for making money but a considerable talent for spending it, or at least losing it. He was fond of poker and other games of chance, which was the chief reason why Mrs. Millay obtained first a separation and then a divorce. She was a woman of great character, as appears upon all the evidence, and set about bringing up her three daughters by her own unaided efforts. The way she chose was that of nursing the sick, a profession in which she soon became so proficient and so greatly in demand that she was always busy. She never was too busy, even so, to pass up music, poetry, and books, which had so real an existence for her that they came very early to dominate the minds of her daughters. Mrs. Millay had somehow or somewhere learned how to write out orchestral parts, so that she was always in demand to get a score ready for the local orchestra in Camden, Maine, the chief of their dwelling places (Rockland, Union, and Camden, but most of all Camden). She could write the score, play the piano, and rehearse the orchestra, which must have made her a fairly essential element in the musical activity of the place.

And thus it was that the daughters, from early years, acquired true familiarity with music. Persons genuinely familiar with music are familiar with all music: they are not pickers and choosers in the earlier stages at all, but take it all as it comes. The little intellectual giant who, at the age of fourteen or fifteen, can only listen to Bach and Stravinsky (and I have met one or two such), is, in my serious opinion, altogether false. Those who really like music and are familiar with it—to whom it is an element in life, like food or climate—may become extremely fastidious in later adult years, although there are few among them who could not joyously revert to some old chestnut treasured in memory, but the great essential for the development of any lifelong association with music is that the relation should be, in all the early phases, as unthinking as possible and consequently almost indiscriminate. My own traffic with music has been almost incessant for nearly half a century, and has led me in time to a considerable amount of intolerance toward much that I once enjoyed, but I am grateful to all the circumstances which made this a late growth—which opened, for many years, literally every door with hardly a difference between them, so that I could delight in the *Christmas Cantata* of Bach without for that reason being insensible to the charms of *La Bohème*. It has always seemed to me that those who truly love music (which includes a surprising number of first-class musicians, too) are far less haughty and superior about it than the intellectuals who only write or talk.

And the Millays were of this kind: as I knew, indeed, from the first surprise of Edna's pianos. Mozart and Beethoven did not, for Edna, exclude anything else: they were summits, but she did not disdain valleys. It was quite obvious whenever music came into question that she had a lifelong acquaintance with practically every sort of musical expression, and felt of each one what was its own particularity. I can still chuckle when I remember how severely she said to me about Brahms' song: "You shouldn't try to sing the *Sapphische Ode*. You haven't got the breath for it." I had, indeed, neither breath nor voice, but it had been an immense pleasure to me for decades to try songs over so as to know them better. This, too, she understood, and endured without a word of complaint some tentative trials of the kind which Esther and I did with Schubert and Schumann: but she drew the line at the *Sapphische Ode*.

She did not, at the time when I knew her, play very well. It is not possible to play the piano well without much daily work, and Edna would allow months to pass without practicing at all. Her hands and fingers were, however, extremely sure and decisive. Her musical instinct was equally affirmative, and her taste or comprehension (I sometimes think they are exactly the same thing) could be depended upon in every reading. Thus, although she played wrong notes and technically failed to achieve what she set out to do, there was never the slightest doubt about the structure, shape, and intent of the composition. To know how a thing goes, what its song is, how it was built in the creator's mind, is proof of a closer communication with music than any technical proficiency in the notes. How often has one heard extremely celebrated pianists perform, with superb skill, works which they do not appear to understand in the least? Offhand, any lover of music can name, at any given moment, half-a-dozen renowned artists who habitually and successfully perform in our concert halls some works (usually masterpieces and therefore considered obligatory) which are beyond their spiritual range in every way.

It was, therefore, a considerable pleasure to hear Edna play even when she had long ceased regular practice. She conveyed music even when she could not play notes. Her whole life had been spent in a relationship of give-and-take with that which can be (when it is) the most truly household art in existence. That was how the three Millay girls grew up: Edna was to have been a concert pianist and Norma a singer, in the sure elections of childhood. And it was the parlor piano in Camden, Maine, that gave them first knowledge of even those complicated forms—such as opera—which can only be heard in big cities.

Edna's work for the stage has scarcely been mentioned here because it has seemed to me outside my chosen limits. She did write, with skill and charm, even as an undergraduate at Vassar, some verse plays which are still performed, although I have seen none of them. *The Princess Marries the Page* was such an undergraduate play in which the young poet played the princess. *Two Slatterns and a King*, which has wit and point in the reading for all its brevity, was another Vassar play. *Aria da Capo*, later on, was acted at the Provincetown Playhouse by the poet's sister Norma, and *The Lamp and the Bell* was a full-length poetic tragedy produced first at Vassar. The stage work which attracted most attention on its first appearance was, however, an opera libretto: *The King's Henchman*, to music by Deems Taylor, produced at the Metropolitan Opera House in 1927.

This opera libretto, even without its music, is an extraordinarily interesting work. I, who have never heard the music, can imagine music when I read it because it was so obviously composed for music. The reader sees in it exactly where Edna wished to give opportunities for lyric or dramatic expressivity in the voices or the orchestra, where she wrote with consideration for vocal variety, where her mind's ear heard contrasts of solo and massed voices, and how she deliberately set out to bring down an operatic curtain. It is a real libretto, a fully realized libretto such as has almost never been written in English. She could scarcely have written it at all without that familiarity with opera which came from the piano in Camden, Maine. This librettist really knew what an opera is.

The King's Henchman has, of course, many other elements of peculiar interest which set it aside from all the rest of Edna Millay's work. In the first place, she deliberately truncated her vocabulary to keep the words within plausible limits for the tenth century in England. This was a difficult experiment both for skill and scholarship, since so much of the English language derives from the Norman Conquest and later: it results in an archaism to which the reader's ears grow accustomed with difficulty. But it has poetic scenes of great beauty in which the poet's chosen difficulty appears to vanish altogether, and others of a bolder and more brutal drama than could be found elsewhere in her work. What strikes me most, however, reading it now so long after its triumphal season at the Metropolitan Opera, is its direct appositeness and effectiveness as a libretto evoking to the imagination (at least to an operagoing imagination!) opera in its entirety. I cannot read it at all as I read either her verse plays or her other poetry—I hear operatic music all through it, and I imagine that she must have heard a good deal while she was writing it.

When I stayed overnight at Steepletop last February, I saw mountains of music here and there—there were always mountains, hillocks, and pyramids of it there—and to my delight, on the top of one pile that caught my eye just as I was going to bed, was a score of *Aïda*. This is the kind of work that only professional musicians, composers, and the general public like: it is not for *dilettanti*, those who can hear nothing but the semi-demiquaver of Beethoven.

"The Millay girls" in Camden, Maine, were not above putting on a performance of *Aïda* for themselves, it seems, with Edna at the piano and Norma and Kathleen singing. These are sometimes the best performances opera ever receives, with no nonsense about one person singing only one part, and such other conventions as handicap the professionals. They are perform-

ances, above all, which stick in the memory, because they are
the ones in which the participating artists, whether they are
twelve or twenty years old, learn for the first time what the thing
means, how it goes, what it is about.

Edna, the eldest, was also the first of the Millay girls to leave
Camden and try her wings. Camden nowadays, with its excellent
little port for pleasure craft as well as fishing boats, is a favorite
seaside resort in summer, with big houses and considerable es-
tates scattered all over the neighborhood. It was so before the
1914-1918 war as well, although perhaps a little less invaded
than it is today. Visitors to Camden are usually told that Edna
Millay had a summer job waiting on tables at the inn; Norma
says it was not Edna, but she herself, who had the job, and that
Edna only came to help out on one evening when there was a
party. In any case, it was at this party, in the summer of 1912,
that Edna was cajoled into reciting some of her poetry. What
she recited was the whole of *Renascence*, a poem which every
person there present must have heard with amazement. (Most
of them probably doubted that she had written it.)

Edna was twenty but undoubtedly looked much younger, as
she did at any age. I have heard descriptions of her schoolgirl
appearance and the ribbon in her hair. The vividness of her
coloring, the extraordinary magic of her voice—all that was
already present. But what must have been the effect of hearing
this girl, little more than a child, reciting as her own a poem
which has not only lyric beauty, a singing line of the rarest grace,
but also form, style, and technical mastery such as we seldom
expect even of mature poets?

In point of fact the poem had already been submitted (by

Mrs. Millay) to a prize contest organized and edited by Mr. Ferdinand Earle for the publisher Mitchell Kennerley, and news had already come that it would be published in the volume issued as a result of that contest. It appeared for the first time in 1912 in *The Lyric Year*, a collection of one hundred poems, but this was still in the future. When Edna recited it that night in Camden it was unknown.

There was among the guests a lady, Miss Caroline B. Dow, who recognized the rare quality both of the poem and of the poet. With her interest thoroughly aroused, she made the acquaintance of the family and offered to defray the expenses of Edna for four years at Vassar College. Mrs. Millay had done her best for her brood, but Vassar would have been beyond her: she accepted with joy.

The Vassar years began to create the wider legend which only a little later developed so fantastically around Edna. The gifted creature, with all her talent and beauty, was bound to stir up the interest of lesser personalities, and she was just enough older than most of them to have an added advantage. She was writing poetry and music, producing plays and acting in them, while most of the other girls were still (as it says in the bird poem) "plodding and walking." The impression she made was ineffaceable for a generation or two in that college, and traces of it will remain for a long time. Vassar women who "saw her once" are nearly always able to describe in every circumstance when and where and how it was, and what she wore, said, or did. And, what is more, the poetry she wrote as an undergraduate at Vassar is a permanent part of her work. Much of it came out in the year 1917 (when she received her degree) as *Renascence and Other Poems*, the volume which made her known to the general public for the first time. Then, three years later, came *A Few Figs from Thistles* (1920), upon which she, too, "awoke one morning to find herself famous."

The years after Vassar, perhaps the first ten of them (1917-1927), are the ones in which Edna Millay can be said to have had her false, or Byronic, vogue. Her truest quality was overlooked or unnoticed by those, far the larger number, who wished for their own reasons to accelerate a *succès de scandale*. The 1920's, in search of a poet laureate, seized upon what suited them amongst her lyrics, and most of all upon the famous quatrain. She was living in Greenwich Village or Provincetown, later in Paris or London or Vienna, and it was a period in which she actually composed some of the best of her lyrics: these, however, were not the ones which most caught the ear of the time. However, she was never again unnoticed; nothing she wrote failed to find a public; she had more than enough encouragement to write badly or not at all if she wished; the world was her oyster. If that particular kind of vogue did afterward decline—as it did, and to the vanishing point—it is my opinion that Edna herself was glad to get rid of it. Her own love for poetry was so deep and true that she turned in upon it more and more for the meaning of her own life and of all life. It was for this that she tended more and more, year after year, to live at Steepletop in her own grove, or among the sea-swept rocks at Ragged Island.

Her marriage to Eugen Boissevain took place at Croton-on-Hudson in 1923, and they bought Steepletop in 1925.

This concludes all that I have to say—indeed all that I know —about her life. Much will be said and written about it, and by persons better qualified than I to do so. There are still a few remarks about her personality as woman and poet which I should like to make, not as an authority upon either, but as one who has beheld in wonder. The principal elements I have emphasized concern her instinctive responses to other forms of life as being related to her own, and chiefly with respect to migratory birds. This, however, is what I saw and say; she never said it. If her behavior was pantheistic, it was a Kantian *als ob*: that is, she behaved *as if* this were her belief and therefore it probably was her belief in the recesses of the consciousness.

But in stressing such an aspect of this rare personality I have perhaps done less than justice to its superb earthiness, its humor, its capacity for ordinary existence, its love of ordinary life. For this reason I have reserved for quotation, by permission of the owner, Mrs. E. P. Lanfranchi of Florida, one of those letters to which I made reference much earlier as "spaghetti letters." Mrs. Lanfranchi is American and her husband, Nino, is Italian, as will appear. Edna writes to them from Steepletop on September 29th, 1937:

Dear Anne and Nino:

What perfect darlings you both are! We've had more fun with that mysterious and marvellous box than I could possibly tell you.

We've had spaghetti four times now, and getting better each time; last night it was flawless, better than any we ever had, except yours. Of course the first time we *did* over-cook it a bit, in spite of Anne's warning, just as she knew we would. You see, at the end of fourteen minutes we tasted it, to see if it was done, which of course was fatal, because it never tastes done until it is mixed with the sauce. So we let it boil a couple of minutes longer. Well, you know. It tasted fine, but it wasn't reserved enough, it had let itself go. Last night, however, it was very high class. We cooked it just under fourteen minutes. Eugen says we have to boil it a minute or two longer here than you do in Florida, because of the altitude,—we're nearly two thousand feet, and of course the water isn't quite so hot when it begins to boil.

The big Parmesan cheese is such fun. And it tastes so much better when you grate it yourself. I'm the grater; and not the tiniest little black speck escapes my hawky eye, or the minutest little hard lump, either.

The rosemary and the origan—are they for flavoring the sauce? We haven't tried them yet, because Anne didn't mention them in her recipe. Of course they're marvellous in other things, soups and dressings for fowls. Herbs get me more excited than anything else that grows, I think. I'm enclosing a post-card to make it easy for you to answer whether or not we should put them in the sauce.

You're always so nice to us. We wanted to do something nice for you, too. But we have no imagination. So I'm sending you a copy of Conversation at Midnight, and my favourite photograph of myself, hoping that if you don't like the one you'll like the other.

Love from us both,

Edna

On a second page, solemnly appended to this by a paper clip, and beautifully typed out by Edna, is the following:

For Nino
(Revised edition of paragraph 2)

We've had spaghetti four times now, and getting better each time; last night they were flawless, better than any we ever had, except yours. Of course the first time we *did* over-cook them a bit, in spite of Anne's warning, just as she knew we would. You see, at the end of fourteen minutes we tasted them, to see if they were done, which of course was fatal, because they never taste done until they are mixed with the sauce. So we let them boil a couple of minutes longer. Well, you know. They tasted fine, but they weren't reserved enough, they had let themselves go. Last night, however, they were very high class. We cooked them just under fourteen minutes.

Her joke about transferring spaghetti into the plural for Nino was one which I, in spite of considerable conceit over my acquaintance with the Italian language, did not get at once; I had to read it over at least twice.

And thus she was, much of the time—blithe and busy, fond of the good things of the world. Many of her oldest friends might think my version of the withdrawn and secret life between birds and poets inexact, and might even fail to recognize it—so various, complex, and at times contradictory are the aspects of such a personality. But amply, abundantly, has she borne it out in the lyrics which she deposited, as the essence of her being, on the rock of time.

A final word must be said about Edna Millay's expressed beliefs in so far as she did express them. I have used words like pagan, pantheist, and metempsychosis, but have been at some pains not to attribute them to her. It is quite clear that she belongs within the Christian tradition, which, after all, in its historic range, has encompassed many variants and comes itself from an older source. Readers of her poetry do not need to be reminded of all the passages in which, from beginning to end, she

expresses either a conscious or an unconscious recognition of
this fact. It may be enough to quote the verses called "The
Little Hill," as being most explicit. (They appeared in *Second
April*, published in 1925 when she was thirty-three.) They are:

> Oh, here the air is sweet and still,
>   And soft's the grass to lie on;
> And far away's the little hill
>   They took for Christ to die on.
>
> And there's a hill across the brook,
>   And down the brook's another;
> But, oh, the little hill they took,—
>   I think I am its mother!
>
> The moon that saw Gethsemane,
>   I watch it rise and set;
> It has so many things to see,
>   They help it to forget.
>
> But little hills that sit at home
>   So many hundred years,
> Remember Greece, remember Rome,
>   Remember Mary's tears.
>
> And far away in Palestine,
>   Sadder than any other,
> Grieves still the hill that I call mine,—
>   I think I am its mother.

She once gave me a little lecture on the historical meaning
and amplification of the word *pietas* which sheds some light on
her thinking, as distinct from her lyric expression, in such mat-

ters. It was at Steepletop in the midst of one of those long con-
versations which I shall never be able to recall in full because
they ranged so wide and far. I had just received some weeks
earlier, and had been playing over and over on the gramophone
in Vermont, the records of the Verdi *Requiem* which were made
in Rome under the leadership of Tullio Serafin and released in
the United States in 1948. We discussed that great work, which
Edna knew as she knew all music, and in the course of the talk
I remarked that one phrase which seemed to me of rare beauty
was that which dominates a long passage for soloists, chorus, and
orchestra about halfway through the *Dies Irae*. The phrase is
"Salva me, fons pietatis." I had been puzzled over a correct translation of *pietas*, since those usually given seem inadequate. Piety,
virtue, mercy, and the like (and above all, pity!) have meanings
more restricted than would seem to be intended by either Verdi's
Requiem or any other work known to me in which the word
occurs.

She declared that these restricted meanings were themselves
all modern, that the process of restriction began in the Middle
Ages, and that in ancient times the word was a very large one
indeed. She quoted Latin poets, but since I do not know them
myself I cannot identify the references, to show that the word
pietas meant the general aspect of a human being's duty to, and
value toward, the world in which he lived—that it was compre-
hensive enough to include almost every functional utility to the
City. The Romans had well-defined notions of what each person's duties were, and only part of these were religious (i.e., to
the official deities). Others were to the family, the state, and to

the virtues esteemed most highly at the time, such as bearing arms. Furthermore, she said, *pietas* could be the objective and not the subjective or intentional result—that is, it could be that which constitutes the final valuable offering of a life, socially considered, and not its temporary efforts. It was, she said, primarily the duty, and ultimately the value, of the man as citizen which determined his *pietas*.

Neither Esther nor I, who listened to this little lecture, knew enough Latin to argue with her, so Edna had her own way. But it occurs to me that if her definitions were correct, the *pietas* of a human life could be that which dwells in the larger world when the single pulse beats no more. It could be song; it could be flight.